The Feisty Woman's Guide to Surviving Mr. Wonderful

The Feisty Woman's Guide to Surviving Mr. Wonderful

Moving on with Humor, Laughter, and Chutzpah!

Elizabeth Allen

THE FEISTY WOMAN'S GUIDE TO SURVIVING MR. WONDERFUL
Moving on with Humor, Laughter, and Chutzpah!

Copyright © 2014 Elizabeth Allen.

Cover design and illustrations by Brittany Barnard
Web design by Weiss Web Designs (weisswebdesign.com)
Website: survivingmrwonderful.com

All rights reserved. No part of this book may be used or reproduced by any means, graphic, electronic, or mechanical, including photocopying, recording, taping or by any information storage retrieval system without the written permission of the publisher except in the case of brief quotations embodied in critical articles and reviews.

The information, ideas, and suggestions in this book are not intended as a substitute for professional legal advice. Before following any suggestions contained in this book, consult your attorney. Neither the author nor the publisher shall be liable or responsible for any loss or damage allegedly arising as a consequence of your use or application of any information or suggestions in this book.

iUniverse books may be ordered through booksellers or by contacting:

iUniverse
1663 Liberty Drive
Bloomington, IN 47403
www.iuniverse.com
1-800-Authors (1-800-288-4677)

Because of the dynamic nature of the Internet, any web addresses or links contained in this book may have changed since publication and may no longer be valid. The views expressed in this work are solely those of the author and do not necessarily reflect the views of the publisher, and the publisher hereby disclaims any responsibility for them.

Any people depicted in stock imagery provided by Thinkstock are models, and such images are being used for illustrative purposes only. Certain stock imagery © Thinkstock.

ISBN: 978-1-4917-5441-2 (sc)
ISBN: 978-1-4917-5440-5 (e)

Library of Congress Control Number: 2014921379

Print information available on the last page.

iUniverse rev. date: 04/22/2015

Contents

Introduction ix

Section 1:
It Really Hurts 1

Chapter 1: The Wallowing Days of Yore: Finish Your Wallow and Move On 3
Chapter 2: Reviving Your Ever-Improving Mental Health 12
Chapter 3: Talking Therapy (This is an easy one!) 23
Chapter 4: Revenge Therapy: No Felonies, Please! 29

Section 2:
Resurrecting the Old/New Me! 37

Chapter 5: Your Appearance – Time For An Upgrade ... 39
Chapter 6: Exercising: Clear Out That Brain Fog and Get Moving ASAP! 47
Chapter 7: Your Nutritional Health . . . Not Your Mental Health 55
Chapter 8: Home Improvements Will Brighten Your Outlook 62

Section 3:
Revival Time for Your Brain 69

Chapter 9: Re-Intellectualizing and Unfreezing Your Brain Cells 71
Chapter 10: Your Job, Your Godsend 78
Chapter 11: It Might Be Time to Become a Legal Eagle 85

Section 4:
Food for the Soul 93

Chapter 12: Sing and Dance All You Want 95
Chapter 13: Get Your Religion Going Again! 102

Section 5:
Moving On 109

Chapter 14: Your New Social Life . . . Or at Least an Attempt at Having One 111
Chapter 15: My Vacation to Sedona 117
Acknowledgments 125

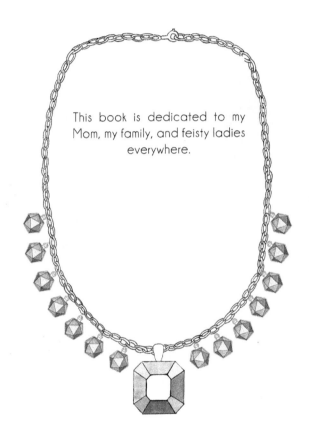

This book is dedicated to my Mom, my family, and feisty ladies everywhere.

Introduction

First you are in shock, then denial, then you cry, then you *scream*!

You cry some more, scream some more, then try to work it out. You ask yourself at least 20 times a day, *Why?* You can't sleep; you blame him, you blame yourself. You try talking, yelling, couples therapy, letters, e-mailing, all to no avail.

He wants to stay in touch to see that you are doing okay. *Okay?* What a slime (the first of many names that you will call him before you settle on the perfect word for him and his behavior: jackass).

He calls to say that he's sorry for what he did. *Sorry?* You ask him to prove it, and of course he can't. Because he can't do what *you* need him to do to repair things. You toss out his leftover clothing, pawn the cheapo jewelry that he gave you, and then after the first year, you *finally* begin to feel better. You start to smile more, laugh more, joke more, and regain your long-lost chutzpah! That 15 pounds you lost is history. You are on your feet ready to live life to the fullest!

Sound familiar? If not, you need to keep reading.

The suggestions included in this humorous yet serious guide to recovery are those that have worked for many middle-aged women. They have been tested many times and can be used and reused over and over again in any frame of mind, either through laughter and with a sense of humor, through your tears, or when you are all alone on those long winter nights.

Whatever course of action you choose from this book, you will get through this fiasco and come out of it a stronger, more vibrant, confident, powerful and totally evolved woman. You regain your chutzpah. You will also be able to look back at your breakup with just the right bit of sarcasm and humor as you move on with your life. The way to your recovery is paved with laughter. No matter how bad you may be feeling right now I know that this book will help you move on. And I kept this thought in the back of my mind, advice given to me by one very wise woman (and there are *many* of them), who reminded me that: "living well is the best revenge".

Because I have lived through a breakup with my very own Mr. Wonderful, I decided to share my story with others. The more I talked to other middle-aged men and women, the more I found that they also had a tale to tell. "I have a good soap opera for you, too," so many said. This book is a journal of those adventures. We all shared our sagas and what we did to move on with our lives. Maybe your potboiler is here. Maybe these words of wisdom will help you cry, laugh, and move on. To move on, to go on with your life after your breakup, is a true testament to the strength of all women. It is my hope that this book will help you begin that process. Special gems of wisdom—"diamonds" I like to call them—will close each chapter. You may not have the jewels right now, but you eventually will, and in your own time and on your own terms.

Read on, feisty woman.

Section 1:

It Really Hurts

Registering the first shock or recognition is the hardest part of the journey. Things may get nastier and more complicated, but they never quite *feel* this bad.

Chapter 1

The Wallowing Days of Yore: Finish Your Wallow and Move On

It started one day with my niggling female intuition. Something was different, but what? Perhaps his behavior? His air of distraction? Sometimes it was a new book, a new cologne, or a new short-term expensive interest—like his sudden taste for fancy Australian red wines when he had always been a microbrewery kinda guy. Just when I thought that I had him figured out, he would swerve in a new direction. The changes were so frequent that I felt like I was being whiplashed. Busy with life and work, I put those thoughts out of my mind for the moment. Some days, though, I just could not shake the feeling that something had really changed, although I had no idea what. After weeks of this sinking feeling, I did some late-night soul searching and started checking out things around the house.

His phone was locked. Never did that before.
Started to lock his briefcase. Never did that before, either.

Then I found this weird female body lotion that my grandmother used in his medicine cabinet. I did not remember seeing him buy that, but it explained his odd new smell. What in the world was going on?

I scanned his checkbook and found visits to a so-called yoga studio that also offered "erotic massage". He wouldn't know a downward-facing dog if it bit him, so what in creation was he doing there? When I asked him about visiting there he vehemently denied it. Looked straight at me—and lied. Never blinked. He just told me a bald-faced lie and didn't even want to know why I would ask such a question.

And then one night I found the receipt. No, *two* of them: a credit card receipt from a restaurant where I knew that we never dined and two ticket receipts to a play that I had always wanted to see. Tried to sleep that night, but to no avail. Went down to the kitchen to our brand new breakfast set at about 6 a.m., where he was calmly drinking his morning coffee, and got the true confession.

It felt like someone had "sucker punched" me in the stomach. It hurt to move, to function, to eat. All I did was cry and shake my head, asking *why*? When a student at school asked me, "Why do you look so sad? You were always so funny"! I knew I had to do something. I needed to take some decisive action.

Strangely enough, I had just recently read the statistics about couples and cheating: 90 percent do not get back together after it's exposed. So, after weeks of soul searching, I decided that I would become part of the 90 percent and get on with my life. That was the most difficult, painful, gut-wrenching decision of my life. Yet I had finally had enough with the self-recrimination and decided to get even. It was time to move on.

But first, I knew I had to stop wallowing in self-pity. Too much weeping and wailing would drive anyone crazy and I did not want to go that route. I tried a variety of first steps and strategies that I'll fill you in on as we go along. Eventually, I decided that the best way to get even—big-time—was to share my story and those of my friends in a book. I would detail the lives of women recovering from their own wallows and living their lives to the max.

In the meantime, though, I spent many months wallowing, moving forward, wallowing, and moving backwards. I read books, saw a therapist, volunteered, kept a journal, and spent much time praying. My volunteering took me to a camp for medically fragile children; to the local prison's children's center; to a home-building charity; and finally returning to a camp in the eastern part of the U.S. where I had worked in my college years. There I served as a resource person with the children and spent my free time with my friend, the camp nurse. She was my summer therapist and what a great listener she was. I related my story to her, along with some of the stories of my friends who were trying to survive their own extended wallows. Somehow, when I related their stories to her, I started to feel better. But she just shook her head and started laughing. "The things we women do to survive!" she said.

And then she advised me to start writing them down, mentioning that she had some friends who would really get a kick out of reading my stories. Why hadn't *I* thought of that? I started with my immediate circle of friends and their stories. Pretty soon I had more stories from their friends, each of whom seemed to know of someone who had been through their very own wallow and had moved on with their sense of humor intact. Almost all of their stories included a certifiable "gotcha" moment for the women who had survived their own Mr. Wonderful. That moment involved perhaps the most important trait that these women possessed: a resilient sense of humor that enabled them to laugh at themselves, not take themselves so seriously, and to move on with their female chutzpah in full swing. These women had reached a point where they felt that enough was enough, and decided to take action—and to take control of their own lives. Their actions can inspire us all never *ever* to settle for anything less than the best in ourselves and in our partners.

We can all learn from each other—and did I ever learn a lot!

Judy, Laura, Janey, and Annie

I spent the first year of my separation in California and gained a lot of insight and support from the women that I met there. After being sad and depressed for months following her separation and divorce, Judy—my fellow menopausal friend from California, with whom I still speak weekly—used her emotional, weepy, hot flash energy to enter law school and become an attorney. She moved on with her life and now counsels women in their divorce cases. She is now in top demand among my separating/divorcing middle-aged women friends. You can move on with your life just like Judy did. You can only cry so much, and then you just get on with it—and getting a law degree doesn't hurt.

My central California walking pal, Laura, decided that she had had enough hurt and sorrow in her life as well. Always one for unconventional medicines and treatments, she first started practicing her yoga daily. She then added meditation. Her goal was to clear out excess baggage from the past, including her own very special Mr. Wonderful. Those memories of and experiences with him were holding her back. She took a deep look inside and knew that she needed some really deep emotional cleaning. She visited an intuitive healer and the rest is history. She got those chakras in alignment, let go of her pain and trained to be a healer herself. Today she shares her gifts with others as an intuitive guidance session healer.

Janey, a middle school math teacher from Modesto, had a jerk of a Mr. Wonderful who could not make up his mind whether to separate, to divorce or to stick around. His decision—of course, not their mutual decision— changed by the week. Janey opened the mail one day, early on in her nightmare, and found the first set of separation papers. When she confronted him with the papers, her Mr. Wonderful shrugged his shoulders and left the room. This continued for months and months. She was in limbo about her life and that of her children. To make matters worse, the November/December holidays were in full swing when things got worse. The day before Christmas he decided to move out. He proceeded to wander about the house deciding what he wanted: this chair, that dresser, you get the drift. Finally unable to find the words to adequately tell off this jerk-wad, her son just straight out said, "Haven't you taken enough already, Dad?" The room went silent and Mr. Wonderful flew the coop on Christmas Eve.

Although their divorce was painful, today they remain just friendly enough for the sake of their kids. Many Christmases have passed since that awful night in Janey's life. She dated his boss and some of his friends, counseled one of his many ex-girlfriends, and now is happily married to a great guy who has three kids to add to her two. Not quite the Brady Bunch, but just as happy.

Annie, a Stockton college dropout, had another tale of woe that would make even the most hard-hearted come to tears. She readily admitted that she had a poor self-image for most of her life and that she was just plain stupid for marrying the first guy who asked her. Turns out that her Mr. Wonderful also had a criminal record, along with some weird interactions with his mother. Because of poor finances, the young couple lived in his family's home. Worse yet, they were so broke they had to borrow money from other relatives. Nothing seemed to be going right for them. Annie did her best to work through their problems, thinking that they were making progress in their relationship and marriage, when she discovered that he had been e-mailing a former girlfriend. When doing the weekly cleaning, she found one of their e-mails that he had been brazen enough to print out. Annie read in horror the words that he had never spoken to her, about how "beautiful, kind, and sexy" she was. Annie's hurt was so acute that she could hardly breathe as she reread the e-mail. When she confronted her Mr. Wonderful, he fessed up and left the room. He never denied it, but found it to be "no big deal".

Almost at her wit's end, Annie left that night, returned to her family, and subsequently divorced her Mr. Wonderful. Her success story? She is now a medical professional, has a great husband and two children, and has survived a serious health crisis. She lives each day with a smile on her face and joy in her heart that her life has been so blessed.

Forgive but Don't Forget

An essential element of ending the wallowing is the "f" word. Not the word that you may have spoken as a noun or a verb when mentioning Mr. Wonderful, but the word *forgiveness*. You get to the point where you have to forgive not because you really don't care anymore, but because you yourself matter more. Remember, as those who were abused as children point out, forgiving is not condoning. It's something you need to do for yourself, not for your abuser. When you can say those three words, "I forgive you", you really are ready to move on. You then become the feisty woman who is ready to share her story and the story of her friends with your own special brand of humor. As the Buddhists say, first you learn how to swim, then you save others who are drowning. So after you learn to "swim", you will begin to empower, uplift, and motivate other women who are stuck in Mr. Wonderful relationships to move forward by creating a life without pain, sorrow, and gloom.

And you will know when the time is right to make that move after reading what follows in this book.

Diamond

My breakup occurred at the beginning of menopause. With all the changing hormones and emotions of that time, I was a total mess and wondered how I would ever stop the hurt, pain, and anguish. I now believe that the "change" gave me the courage, confidence, and guts to finally stand up for what was best for *me*. Imagine that! I am important and special. We all need to feel that way on our own, and don't need anyone to tell us that. It did take me a while to figure that one out after many years of negativity and gloom.

Chapter 2

Reviving Your Ever-Improving Mental Health

If you've gotten to the forgiveness stage, you are truly on the road to recovery—even though many days do not feel that way. Trust me, you are. If you have cut off contact with your ex, changed your home phone number, email address, and yes, even the cell phone number, and returned his mail to sender, you are really on the way. It is now just you, so, what do you do when the blues hit you out of nowhere? (And believe me, they will). You just go with it and this too shall pass. Feel whatever you need to, cry whenever you need to, and eventually those moments will become fewer and farther between. That day could not have come soon enough for me, so check out the following series of strategies for continuing on that bumpy, ever-changing, sometimes too-long road to feeling like yourself again. Your focus right now needs to be on *you*. So here's what you can do.

The women included below are from my California divorce support group. Thanks, ladies, for your insight, support, and of course your tissues.

See a therapist. Jess contacted her work EAP (Employee Assistance Program) and started out with a therapist who would have been better suited for a more demure, well-mannered woman. She ultimately found a new therapist named Alison, who shared her bawdy sense of humor and desire for revenge. Alison had Jess call her doctor and set up an appointment to help her live with the stress of her divorce. The doctor recommended antidepressant drugs to calm her down so that she could function and keep her job—and they really helped. "Healing Through Pharmaceuticals should be a bumper sticker; they can make the day float by," said Jess who can attest to the fact that there is no shame in needing help with your life. But you should think of prescription drugs as a transitional stage: a raft to get you across the river, but not something to carry around on your back forever. Today Jess is pharmaceutical-free—and happy to be free of her Mr. Wonderful to boot. (If you don't have the resources for a therapist, well, that's what friends are for, as we'll see below).

Keep a journal. This is a lot less expensive than therapy and just as helpful for maintaining mental (and physical) health. It's a therapeutic way to work through your anger and get *all* of the buried feelings out. Release them with a sigh-filled good-bye and feel your heart open up and your body relax a bit as they go. You'll come to look on your journal as a true friend and confidant, one who will never break a date or cancel dinner because "something came up". No matter how much we may confide in a friend, partner, parent, or even a professional counselor or therapist, there is something unfiltered about the experience of engaging in conversation with your deepest self. After you are ready to move on, burn those journals. You really would not want anyone else to read them, now would you? They could be really scary. (Better yet, put them in a locked box or password-protected file so you can read them a year from now and see how much progress you've made).

Eventually you will be ready to add to your journal writing one of the Native American smudge pot ceremonies that will cleanse all negative energy (i.e., him) from your home. Sounds a bit far-fetched, but people I know who have tried it swear by it. Try a smudge pot with lavender, lemon, sage, and cedar to further get rid of all of your ex and the negative energy he exuded in your journal writing and in your life with him. As you light this mixture and add your journals to the fire, the smoke will attach to all of the bad energy and it will float away. As the smoke clears, all the negative energy is removed and someday will be regenerated into positive energy: your journals will also be history. If it works for the Native Americans it will work for you. Be sure to have a well-ventilated area out of doors. No home fireplace will work. One of my friends, Kara, nearly set fire to her living room and set off all of the smoke alarms in her house. No one needs that kind of that stress as you are endeavoring to get rid of your Mr. Wonderful stress.

Did I mention that *cough therapy* helps too? Sounds strange, but five coughs twice a day really do work. Get him *totally* out of your being in any way that works for you. Better coughing and scribbling in a journal than venting in public. Some research says that you cough because you are dehydrated—probably from all that crying. Other people attribute colds and coughs to negative energy, feeling repressed, or the bottling up inside of tears. This was definitely not me. I tried the cough therapy technique and I am proud to say that I have not had a cough or serious cold in years. I wonder why? Yet another daytime TV personality said that as you cough you get rid of the emotional baggage of not being your own boss. I still cough daily but smile when I think of how much better my life is without Mr. Wonderful and his baggage in my life.

Keep on talking as long as people will listen. You will really find out who your friends are now. If they can still be patient with you and your temporary lapses of sanity, they will be your friends forever. If they keep telling you to just move on, then move on from being their friend. Better to lose a friend than your sanity. A friend is one who truly understands when you need to talk (and believe me, you will need their understanding for a long time). Most middle-aged women have restless nights of sleep anyway. My choir friend Michelle and I had a signal: three rings, cough when the machine picks up, and then hang up.

Within ten seconds of hanging up, she was calling to check in on me. Sometimes she even fell asleep when we were talking, and so did I. Somehow I felt less alone and always connected to someone who actually seemed to care about my well being. Eventually we discovered melatonin and now both sleep better through the night. But when the nearly obsolete answering machine picks up a call, I smile and remember her kindness.

Reconnect with your neighbors. They may have thought you were stuck-up or standoffish. (No wonder they did. You never knew about all of the invites to their houses, because Mr. Wonderful forgot to tell you! Or you were too busy spending "quality time" with him to drop by for dinner or a party). My neighbor Mary has been a Godsend. She felt that I was always a bit snooty, bitchy, and pompous. However, she recognized "the look" on my face and knew immediately what I was going through. When we later spoke about missed dinners and party invitations, Mary uttered some choice Irish terms of endearment and from then on we were friends. She has always checked in on me, lent a sympathetic ear, and let me really vent about a certain Mr. Wonderful who used to be in my life. She and her friends also joined in on the male bashing as we all shared a good laugh and many, many glasses of wine. She remains a close friend today.

Surround yourself with children. They see things clearly and honestly and won't hold back about how they really feel. The kids in your neighborhood are always lurking for food and drinks. Reward them for being patient as you ignored their earlier pleas. It will also help to keep your windshield safe during softball and flag football games. They will remember you when selling Girl Scout cookies, wrapping paper, candy, and gourmet food. You will really eat well. My younger cousin also had many words of wisdom for one so young. She said it best when she remarked that if he makes you cry, then he is not worth it. No one, she said, should ever make you cry. Wow. Words so profound from one who sees it like it really is. She was five years old at the time and continues to be an important person in my life.

Read something. I am a big reader of all things in print, and feel out of it if I don't read the newspaper everyday—and do the crossword. Studies show that this keeps the brain cells working. Yours have been slightly numbed lately, so get them moving with that daily puzzle. If it works for the seniors, it can work for you, too. Note: *Do not,* however, read the obituaries. I heard about a lady in California named Dawn, who came across the obit of her former boyfriend—only to learn that he happened to still be married while they were dating. She thought about ratting him out to his widow, but decided that she got the better part of the deal anyway. That story was a hit with my divorce support group.

Volunteer for something totally different. I have worked with the female incarcerated population and their children for years. My tale of woe was nothing compared to what these women and their families were going through; 25 to life is a long time to be separated from your family for one stupid action in your life. It did wonders for my psyche, and prevented me from doing something stupid for revenge (that chapter comes later) when I witnessed what their lives were like. Many studies have shown that when you are feeling low, nothing does more for your self-esteem than helping others. As my Dad always said, "someone is always worse off than you are". He said those words many times throughout his life, but they were especially poignant in the last weeks of his life. Just check out local volunteer services; they always need help. Working with seniors was particularly worth my while as the older gents flirted with me and made me feel special again. Take your compliments *wherever* you can get them. I volunteered to help out with bingo at a senior center. Those folks may be old but they are really competitive and take their bingo very seriously. You need to on your toes for that one.

Taking in a movie would be a great start. Many things are out there for you to do on your own, but after being a couple for so long, you just need some guts to try them. That first time can be daunting for obvious reasons. My fellow support group attendee Rose felt that everyone was watching her, but then looked around and saw that many others were on their own, too. She knew that she could laugh, burp, cry, or moan whenever she wanted; she did not embarrass anyone because she pretended that the person behind her did it. Local papers may alert you to pre- and post-movie discussion groups as well. Sometimes you even discuss the movie over a great meal. Talk if you want or just eat. Another woman interviewed in the local newspaper found also that these after-film discussion dinners in her area were a great way to meet new people. Some city restaurants are now offering sections for those who are eating solo. Just turn and chat to your neighbor and keep it cool; sure beats the local singles bar, a place where many older singles would never be caught dead. Most middle-aged women that I know, did the bar crawl in their 20's and are never going back there again.

Nor do you need to limit yourself to restaurants, which can get expensive after a while. Twice-divorced Dina joined a hiking group and gained her waist back, along with a new appreciation of the outdoors; at a women's conference that I attended she spoke of her struggles and how hiking had changed her life. Your local library probably has a forum where authors and activists speak and then lead a discussion. The same goes for artists' associations and book clubs. Going to a gallery opening can feel artificial, just like trying to meet someone at a museum, but the free wine does tend to make people more convivial, and a discussion gives you the chance to start a conversation with others in the crowd. I find that if you go to these events not looking to "meet" the right guy, but just to have some fun, expand your mind and your social group, you have more of a chance to make friends with members of either sex.

Watch the sun set. I have been taking pictures of sunsets for a long time. I live on a beautiful hill where they can be absolutely breathtaking. I always have my 35mm camera, iPhone, or digital camera in my bag ready to capture their color, shapes, and the sheer drama of the end of the day. The pictures remind me that I have made it through yet another, sometimes emotionally fraught day, with the promise of a brighter tomorrow. Sound like a script for a Hallmark card? Who cares: because I've got the pictures to go with those beautiful scenes of nature that can lift my spirit every day. Wherever you live, find a place nearby where sunsets are visible, even if it requires a short walk or going into a different room of your house or apartment. The trick is remembering to notice when the time is approaching. You will instantly feel much better knowing that despite your sadness, these gorgeous sunsets may be cheering up another person with the same sadness, grief, and heavy heart as you.

Smile as much as you can. Say that you will smile at least 100 times a day, from those first steps in the morning (that would be two already) to the last ones at night. Count and see how soon you get to 100. It will surprise you and uplift your mood at the same time. Smile at upbeat, positive, funny things only. Research shows that smiling improves your health, eases your stress, and improves your overall appearance. Just walk down the street and start smiling at people. Seniors really respond to this—and who knows if one of these fellow "smilers" might have an eligible son or grandson. (A little early for these thoughts I admit, but why not? At the very least you might make a new friend). You will feel more attractive, lower your blood pressure, and appear to be more confident. Perhaps most important you will be helping yourself to stay positive, a feeling not present at the first stages of your separation blues. Deandra, one of my divorce support friends who offered all of us makeover tips and new hairstyles forced herself to take this smile test and it changed her life. First she started out with a smile. She then compelled herself to stay positive by not thinking any negative thoughts. Some days that was really tough, but you can't smile and be negative at the same time, so something's gotta give. When she was smiling, her message of "Life is Good" drew people to her. She found a rewarding new job as a home health aide and from there went on to finish her nursing degree. She continues to stay away from depression, stress, and worry by smiling. Who would have thought that something as simple as smiling could have changed her life? In effect, she was taking a perfectly legal natural drug that has only positive side effects. Today she works in a nursing home and brings her smile to the seniors there. And, yes, one of them did have a grandson who is now Deandra's significant other.

However, resist smiling at someone or something that won't help you reach your goal. Smashing a bug or killing a bee does *not* count as something that makes you smile. Revenge smiling definitely does not count and will make you feel worse later on.

Finally, do at least one new thing every month. Remember that you are now free to do new things. Buy some red shoes. Take a really long walk in the rain. Test drive a Ferrari (my next big birthday goal). Get a pet. Get some fish. See a new Broadway show. Take a vacation to some place that you have always wanted to see. Buy an expensive handbag. Plant a flower garden. Learn to bake. Redo your home décor. Invite a friend to a concert. Call an old friend and catch up. I could go on, but you get the idea.

Diamond

Develop a mantra that helps you feel better. This one took a while. At first when I repeated it, my answer was, "Yeah, right." But today it does make me feel better. My mantra goes something like this: "I am a beautiful, funny, smart, kind, generous woman and I deserve all of the great things that life has to offer". Create your own. This one is already taken.

Chapter 3

Talking Therapy
(This is an easy one!)

Talk therapy is easy because it's what we women do best. More than one news source has commented on this revealing communication statistic: women use an average of 100 words in their everyday conversations, while men use just 70. Women have 3 a.m. talk-and-cry binges with their friends; men just snore. I could continue, but you get my point. Talking out your revenge ideas with friends may feel really great, but remember the power of karma before you start putting those fantasies into action.

Still, I read about Lisa in one of my women's magazines. Lisa felt especially feisty and empowered one day, so she called up her ex's new girlfriend. What an eye-opening conversation that was. She really got more information than she bargained for. Even though Lisa's Mr. Wonderful had been cheating on her with the new gal, he was apparently now cheating on the new gal with another new gal. The best part of all this talking is that Lisa and the new—now old—gal became friends.

After completing a near hour-long "talk session" with my Pennsylvania college friend Sheri about her relationship issues, I know that talk therapy truly makes all women feel better. A wise woman once told me that women use too many words. Not with each other, however, but with the male species because it has been my experience that men can absorb only small doses of verbiage at a time. Their brains are simply wired for eating and sex, not for much else, especially not for talking or listening to us. Those two other subjects always seem to get their attention even if our words don't.

So talk, talk, and talk some more to recovery. Have friends lined up who can take your call around the clock. I read about another woman in a magazine who never knew when the urge to purge would occur. Three in the morning was often a good time for her, but she usually fought off the urge until the next morning. Not always, though. Once during a 3 a.m. call, she managed to clear her brain only to fill someone else's with doubts about her partner and his behavior. The next night she was finally getting some sleep when she got *her* 3 a.m. call. So she suggests that you set a deadline time for calling and have your friends stick to it. Instruct them to ignore you after 11 p.m. Then maybe we can all get enough sleep.

But you also have to know where to draw the line even in your daytime talkfests. Despite what I've said about the benefits of talk therapy, I speak from experience when I say that you will be able to take only so much of the fellow wallowing and sadness. This may sound like a paradox, but as in so much of life, balance is the key. After reading a "lessen your stress" divorce tip to this effect in a magazine,

I began to shy away from seeking the comfort of others who were going through their own separations or divorces. I decided to give myself a six-month vacation from nonstop pity parties, and at least get to the point where I wouldn't think about my breakup for two hours at a stretch. When I shared this article with my divorce group, I was glad to discover that we were all tired of each other's bitching and moaning. We agreed to limit our whining sessions to 10 or 15 minutes at our meetings and then move on to more uplifting topics.

As stated earlier, I might also suggest that you seek out a good counselor. Mine actually rescued me more than she will ever know. She allowed me to express the full gamut of feelings, something I was never "allowed" to do in my relationship. I once saw her four times in a week. How's that for support? She was also available by phone and shared my sense of humor, my anger, and my sarcasm. I continue to have monthly "tune up" sessions. An experience like this truly takes time, time, and more time to recover. Seeing a therapist is not a sign of weakness, but of strength—the strength to get help, to move forward with your life. She will always be there to cheer you on.

Read all of the self-help books that you can stand, but stop when they all start sounding the same. After a while they just made me cry, feel worse, or feel a false sense of hope when I knew deep down that there was none. I knew that I had been reading too many of them when I went to a book signing for a new novel and the author asked me about the best book that I had read recently. I was speechless (something new for me) and it hit me that I really needed to move on and to cut the self-help words, sayings, and mantras from my vocabulary. This author's novel was just what I needed, a mystery potboiler about love and murder. And yes, the heroine persevered and triumphed in the end.

Talk to yourself everyday. Look in the mirror and smile when you do it. The best pep talk that you may get is from *you*. Mara brought an article to our divorce group that included some cheesy yet useful sayings, verses, poems, and the like, which I pasted around my bathroom medicine cabinet. I could hardly see the mirror in the bathroom and my wall looked like it had been wallpapered in sticky notes. They always seemed to get stuck to my feet when I got up in the middle of the night for my 4 a.m. constitutional. You may remove and store them away when you are ready to move on. Found the box when I was doing my yearly house cleaning this week. I just smiled and decided to keep them in case another friend just might need them.

As I said earlier, even we women get talked out and need a rest from it. So pick up the pen and the notebook and start writing. You will be surprised what you can write down, but maybe were never able to speak. Never ever reread what you written if you're still going through a break-up. Fold over the page to resist that temptation. Besides, those words could *really* scare you at a later date. There will come the day when you will actually have a nice little bonfire in your back yard because you might die from embarrassment if someone other than you ever read them. This is not essential, and you may want to keep some of them to read later, but not always. I performed a special ceremony burning them with herbs that were to cleanse my house from the bad spirit of Mr. Wonderful, as mentioned earlier. That felt great, but I wondered what my neighbors were thinking as I had my little bonfire behind my condo. They noticed a change in my mood and said nothing. Must have been a sight as I set this fire at 1 a.m. on a Saturday.

Diamond

Today I am still keeping a journal. I include at least five major events of my day and how I turned lemons into lemonade. Once I have written my thoughts down I never read them again. Time to move on even in journal writing.

Chapter 4

Revenge Therapy:
No Felonies, Please!

Keep in mind that everyone wants to give you advice, and not all of it is valuable or even viable. Listen to the advice of *true* friends only—and by this point you will know who they are. Follow only the advice that prevents you from committing a felony. A paralegal in my lawyer's office helped me out a great deal with this one. Always wait at least one or two days after you have discussed a particularly nasty revenge tactic before you decide whether to do it. The karma could come and get you, too. Chances are also that his new chicklet wouldn't believe a word that you said about him anyway, but a few years down the road she probably will. These guys don't change; they just move on to another unassuming victim. Clothing can always be replaced, but your life really is a pretty good one so hang on to it.

However, the local cop in the town where I once taught school informed me that thanks to former President Bush (I cannot believe that I am saying this because I thought that the man was totally ineffective), the Patriot Act made stalking legal. You can actually stand within 12 feet of someone's house and tape record those inside without their reporting it to the police—all in the interest of national security. This is a useful tidbit for the potential felon in all of us (but keep in mind that it's also legal for your ex).

Otherwise, though, the possibilities are endless. As a lawyer, Jackie discovered what utilities could legally be canceled, and knew just what to say to Mr. Wonderful's boss when he called that would make his life miserable. She cleaned out the bank accounts, canceled the credit cards, and had the locks changed faster than you could say, "Don't get mad. Get even".

I also marveled at a famous TV personality's sister's remedy for her cheating, soon-to-be ex-husband. It seemed that he wanted to take lots of the home furnishings as he was about to leave their home of more than 25 years. She decided that one of the items that he was not getting was the bed. She went to the garage, got out the safety glasses, cranked up his chainsaw, and sliced their bed into little bits—mattress and all. The only thing the bed was good for after that was pillow stuffing. (Don't know if he took that along with him, though).

One very wise woman named Kay, who always seemed to have many sage words to say in her work as a successful intuitive healer, described revenge this way: *The best revenge is a great life!* What a simple yet profound statement that really says it all. Moving on with your life, having your own retirement, your own home, your own peace of mind, and your own friends makes the revenge mode disappear sooner than you can say, He is such a jackass, idiot, moron, and other words not to be mentioned in this book. Once you have vented with all those words, you will feel better. Soon they will fade from your vocabulary and you can begin attracting the man of your dreams. My Mom always said that you attract more good things with honey than vinegar. You will know when you are ready for this.

If you're feeling bold, you may even want to contact some of Mr. Wonderful's exes. I met Janice in a New York airport. She and I started to chat and she, too, had a story to tell. She called her ex's ex-wife, who turned out not to be nearly as awful as Mr. Wonderful had claimed she was. Janice was not only able to fill in his backstory, but also got some shockers in the process, so comparing notes really helped. Maybe Janice wanted to hear some of her revenge tactics (we all do whether we want to admit it or not). The satisfaction of sharing her feelings with another who had been treated badly by him was good for Janice—and for the ex-wife. And trust me, Janice might someday get calls from one or more of her successors. By then, she will be able to shake her head, smile and thank her lucky stars that he is out of her hair and her life for good. Both gals are stronger women with a connection to each other that Mr. Wonderful never could have imagined. They have stayed in contact, sharing their stories of their ever-evolving love lives.

Peggy, part of a huge Boston Irish family, has remained friends with her ex's family and always will be. She grew up with her Mr. Wonderful's relatives, and they were all friends long before he came on the scene. How he felt about this was no concern of hers. She did agree on one common point with his family: *not* to discuss him and his (mis)adventures in any way, shape, or form. Peggy at first really had struggles with this one, but then decided that she could never have too many friends in this life, so she put him and his misery behind her, and continued their friendships, which are still going strong today. If they wanted to be a part of her life she just looked at it this way: you are keeping the best parts of him and discarding the crappy ones. Seems that women make friends and keep them no matter what. She kept them and got rid of him.

The really important thing in all this is to keep karma in mind. Read all you can about it. Even listen to John Lennon's song "Instant Karma". Too much revenge thinking keeps him in your thoughts and in your world of dizzying emotions. Plot a few revenge plans and then move on. Linda, a friend from exercise class, thought often about this, yet she wondered just how much revenge she could really exact (do not answer that one). Sometimes it felt like there was never enough, but then she remembered the words of a wise male friend of hers (and we do have many of them): "remember that what goes around comes around". Too many nasty deeds will bounce back and be yours if you continue in the revenge mode too long. Linda had enough to deal with right now, so she kept the tactics at a minimum before they *really* could get her into trouble. Fantasies are one thing, but the reality could be worse. No boiling rabbits á la *Fatal Attraction* for her.

Rosey, a New York City social services agency worker, took her revenge tactic one step further: she decided *never* to speak of him by name. It gave her the power of removing just one more part of him from her life. She developed some new names that she can say in public. Your friends might not even need a name because when you begin speaking about Mr. Wonderful, your face, your voice, and your entire affect simply change and show the pain and anguish (which incidentally will soon become relief) that you still feel over your breakup. The less you speak of him the better. Besides, you will eventually decide that enough is enough and get on with your life. Now *that* is truly the best revenge of all. There are plenty of other guys to spend your time thinking about.

We all know that what we really want at first is revenge. We all think, "How dare that _____ do something like that to me? I deserve to be treated so much better than this. I am a good person and have tried my best to be there for him and to work hard at our relationship. He never seemed to care about anyone but himself". And the list goes on and on. Does this sound familiar? We all have these feelings, sometimes so intense that we can hardly breathe. The anger wells up inside and you just want to do something—anything—to make it go away. The strategies below have worked for my friends and may be just what you need to move on.

Speaking of Tactics

Here (not in any specific order) are some of the more clever stratagems that have been shared with me by men *and* women in the same recovery mode. You can use any of them if you want, or just get a good laugh out of them.

1. Toss out all of his clothing. Where you toss it is up to you. On the lawn, along the highway, or toss it at him and aim low. Once it is out of your house, you will feel so much better. Stop along the interstate and toss his things in the woods or give all of his suits, ties, and dress shoes to a homeless shelter.

2. Give any leftover things to the Goodwill store and get a tax credit. You have earned it, that's for sure.

3. *Have a dish smashing party.* Invite a couple of friends to your house, attach a giant sheet of plastic to the wall, get a bottle (or two or three) of wine, and place all the dishes that he ever touched nearby. One by one have your female guests toss the dishes that he used at the wall. Wine will be required to enjoy the total experience. A short insulting comment preceding each toss is required followed by cheers and giggles and laughing. But *please* remember to warn your neighbors that the party is going on. Better yet, invite them to join your little gathering.

4. *Save a few pieces of his clothing to rip to shreds when you are reminded of something really stupid or annoying that he did.* This helps get the frustration out of your system and will yield multiple car cleaning rags in the process. What a great use of his clothing. As the months pass and you still keep finding things, just toss them in a bag and call a charity. You can still get the satisfaction of knowing that your tossing him and his things out was the right decision for you.

5. *Get creative with valuable pieces of furniture such as a coffee table.* Saw up the coffee table into little coasters and give them to your friends as Christmas gifts. At least the table will come in useful to you.

6. *Soak all of your ex's electronic devices in water.* Place them carefully in rows in the bathtub and turn on the hot water tap. In addition remove all of the buttons from his shirts, disable the zippers, and cut holes in all of his socks.

Diamond

Just keep remembering the mantra that Linda used, but think of it both ways: "What goes around comes around." This truly does reflect how life seems to evolve. Good deeds return to you, but so do bad ones. *Choose wisely*, my feisty friends.

Section 2:

Resurrecting the Old/New Me!

The worst has come, but now it's time to reach deep down inside and start the long, confusing process of remembering who you used to be and then making yourself even better.

Chapter 5

Your Appearance –Time For An Upgrade

You may not feel like even moving or getting out of bed. You may not want to take a shower or eat anything but dark chocolate! But let's face it. Sooner or later you will have to leave your self-imposed cocoon of home/couch/bed and go out into the world. Look in the mirror and gaze deeply into your raccoon-looking eyes. You will see a small glimmer, just a glimpse, of that great woman you know is in there. Appearance really counts because if you look great you will begin to *feel* great. Well, maybe not great, but at least a teeny bit better. We all know that clothes make the woman, so what better way to revamp your wardrobe and upgrade your self-esteem at the same time? What are you doing with those 20 credit cards anyway?

First, discard *all* of the things that he bought for you. My friend Jodi, a New York City police lieutenant, had a mountainous pile. Her favorite sexy black sweater started her pile of toss outs. Yuck! It still smelled like him. She promptly tossed it in her Goodwill pile. "Let some other woman smell his cologne," she said. Jodi reasoned that he had bought that sweater on sale anyway and he probably used her coupon, too (never could remember to bring his own coupons, now could he?). She resisted the urge to shred everything when she realized that she could get a tax deduction for donating all of his left-behind clothing. Jodi put that money from her tax refund to good use and took a spa weekend getaway with two friends. Isn't "payback" great?

She then shared with me her own 12 Step program:

Step 1: To start, discard at least 5 to 10 items. If you can't imagine why she picked 5 or 10 just bend over those fingers and it will come to you. Jodi really enjoyed ripping 5 to 10 more items from the hangers, stopping to bid each one a fond farewell.

Step 2: Wait 15 minutes and go at it again. Discard 5 more. Now Jodi's closet started to breathe again and so can you! She could actually see what great clothing she had picked out for *herself*. She kept her purchases only and still had a closetful of stylish clothing to wear. You go girl.

Step 3: Start to match up the leftover items if possible. At this point, Jodi realized that although she liked her clothes, nothing matched. She would have looked better going out in her PJs, which she did on more than one occasion. She knew that she was in trouble when she started to look like the middle school students that she saw at the mall. "Time for retail therapy," she said.

Step 4: Jodi discovered that she had to write down what she needed. Lists and more lists; they really kept her organized and on task. Another friend of Jodi's advised her to used her old love letter envelopes to make her lists while having quite the bonfire with the cards, letters, and poems from Mr. Wonderful. This is poetic justice at its best.

Step 5: Create 5 outfits to start. Better yet, purchase 10 new outfits symbolic of her Step 1 mood. Those fists have come in really handy for Jodi and her fiery personality. And why not use both of her fists and the number 10 to benefit herself even though she would rather have used them on— oh, never mind. Jodi always kept us apprised of her use of the number 10 and we always caught her drift. Any number could be your own symbolic, lucky number as long as you use it to spruce up your new look. She dressed up even on her bad days. Over time her new look enabled her to be the fashion diva of her entire floor at work, attracting many new dates for her.

Step 6: To Jodi, new shoes were also a must—but no black shoes for her. "Try a red pair, bright blue, something totally out of character," she said. A splash of color in her wardrobe gave her the smile that she needed to brighten up her day every time she glanced down at her spiffy new shoes. She still refuses to buy black shoes. A new purse also went a long way with Jodi. She made sure that it was big enough to hold all those tissues that she needed at first, but now it holds her outfits for yoga classes or a weekend getaway. (We'll cover that in a future chapter). And since the make-up department was right next to the purse department, Jodi stopped by for a makeover. Plenty of department store sales women are ready and very willing to help you out with this venture. Jodi's new make-up also helped cover up her temporarily red, puffy raccoon eyes. She now looks like a new woman and ten years younger according to all of her friends.

Step 7: It was probably haircut-and-color time about now, too. Jodi went for a new color and a new look. She got a style and color she liked and that felt good for her. Her ex always helped choose her hair color so she decided that she now needed to change her new look on her own terms. Jodi took her own sweet time looking through the styling magazines, but not so long as to drive the salon people crazy. The stylists and colorists gave her advice that turned out to be much cheaper than her therapist. And they were pretty good at this. She took a picture before she started and another one at the finish. We were all astonished at how great she looked. We begged her to send the before and after pictures to a women's magazine; she wanted to post it in a billboard on the way to her ex's work. Fortunately, she just posted it on Facebook.

Step 8: New bras and underwear were a must. "Time to lift up those puppies and flaunt your shape," said Jodi. She knew that she was a stunning broad even if he never told her so. She had a bra fitting that enhanced her assets even though she had gone in feeling that she pretty much lacked *any* assets in any capacity. "Stand up straight and look confident and in control," she barked at all of us. "We women can all be great actresses if we want to", and with her leading us we truly were.

Jodi next moved to her undies, which under no circumstances should ever be of the granny variety, no matter what your career. Jodi chose something a bit more daring, but avoided any underwear that caused her more stress and aggravation than she already had in her life. She really could not stop tugging at a thong (it always seems to get lost or stuck somewhere). She tried to go for something comfortable, yet slightly sexy, even though she felt totally unsexy some days. This too will pass. Jodi eventually elected to "go commando" (sans undies) on occasion, but that is another story.

Step 9: Perhaps, Jodi decided, she had not been seeing her ex clearly (and it's really painfully obvious that she was not) so she scheduled an eye exam as well. Her new frames made her face look less strained, de-emphasized her red nose, and covered up and drew attention away from her red eyes. She got Gaga-style sunglasses as well. They really helped cover up her recuperating eyes and nose while adding an air of mystery to her appearance. A new shape, color, and style will go a long way to bringing back the great you that has been buried for years and years. She looked the femme fatale part without committing any crimes (that we know of).

Step 10: With our help, Jodi next moved to her jewelry box. She took out all of the jewelry that he'd ever bought her. *All of it!* Jodi put it in a box and let it sit for a few months with her sister. She resisted the urge to flush it or toss it out the window (as she should have done with all of his things, she said). After a few months, she pawned her jewelry only to find out how cheap he really was. The amount it was worth truly shocked her, but she did have enough for a weekend trip to the Holiday Inn with the ladies. I think that the staff was very happy when we left on Sunday morning.

Step 11: Before our Holiday Inn soiree, a manicure and a pedicure were a must for Jodi. Red nails and toes reminded her of the blood that she wanted to draw from him, but she really couldn't at this point without getting into trouble. She could just imagine ways to this, but this guy was definitely not worth any more of her thoughts and time. The manicure and pedicure added a frame of sorts to her appearance and a nice shine and sparkle to her new life. The color she chose was one that no words can even describe except to say that it was rarely used at the salon, only maybe by a serial killer.

Step 12: For future reference, buy a new little black dress and dressy shoes when the urge strikes you. You never know when you may need them. Turns out that Jodi wore just that to her first New Year's Eve party as a single woman. She had the time of her life even without Patrick Swayzee. She had been cutting out pictures of dresses from women's magazines and looked at them for six months just trying to get a new look. Her tastes definitely changed. She has also changed as well. But her little black dress has enabled her to be the classic doll we all knew that she would always be.

Jodi reminded us all that just trying on a new outfit would definitely lift your spirits. "Check yourself out in the mirror," she said. "You are probably looking better now than ever because complimenting *you* was never his strong suit. The fact that you know you look great is *all* that really matters at this point".

Finally, Jodi reminded us all to smile as much as we could. Although at first your smile may have the appearance of cramps or of being punched in the stomach (it really *does* feel like both at the same time), it can signal the start of your recovery! Smile away! Pretty soon you will begin to smile more than you have been crying. Give it time, but you will truly appreciate that he is out of your life. Yes, Jodi, you are right about that one.

Diamond

Time now to go out and enjoy life. Even short trips out without crying build up your confidence and give you a medium to show off the new you! Visit the bookstore, go to a movie, go any place that will get you out of the house. Imagine just how great you will look with those new undies, shoes, hairdo, manicure and pedicure, new glasses, and a new attitude. You may be surprised at how good you *do* look, and that alone will make you feel a teeny bit better. One day at a time will lead to a stronger, more confident and happier you. You go woman.

Chapter 6

Exercising: Clear Out That Brain Fog and Get Moving ASAP!

You need to exercise to keep your body in great shape and your brain fog-free. You probably have always considered yourself to be in fairly good shape. You have also probably embraced some sort of regular exercise and watched what you ate for as many years as you can remember. (I also believe that a healthy diet can help us handle the stresses and bumps that life sends us, and I'll get to that in a subsequent chapter). The problem is that when you're going through the emotional duress of a breakup or divorce, it's easy to forget about maintaining the routines that have kept you healthy all along. Now more than ever you need to remember that just getting out and moving gets those endorphins going, and when they are going you feel so much better. Those bad moods are a little easier to handle when you are exercising. Counting steps, watching the scenery, and looking out for speeding vehicles really does keep your mind otherwise occupied. Those exercise scientists know what they are talking about.

Lori, a friend from my second divorce support group (yes, I needed more help than I thought, so I joined yet another group after my six-month relapse into wallowing and incessant crying), decided that credit card swiping was its own form of "exercise". She practically sprinted from store to store in the mall as she completed a makeover similar to Jodi in chapter 5. She also joined a gym and learned karate, took up target shooting, and tried yoga (although she started to freak everyone out with her truly unusual yoga poses). Seems that any form of exercise helped her brain fog start to lift sooner, confirmed to us all, after she dropped the pharmaceuticals and removed her "Live the Joy of Pharmaceuticals!" bumper sticker from her car. Lori also decided that regular exercise was much cheaper than credit card "exercise" and has not renewed any of her shredded cards.

Something as simple as a walk has advantages. Another new fellow divorcee, Lena, the dog lover in my new circle of recovering divorcees, had always taken her dogs on long walks before and after work. It kept her dogs regular and her sweet tooth under control. On one of those daily treks she met the man she would marry. Who says that a dog is man's best friend? Seems to apply to women, too. Now she is walking with the dogs and her new husband, preferring their company to that of her ex-husband. And yes, her brain fog has cleared, too.

A local school librarian, Marian's new mantra is: "Exercise every day in one form or another." Walk, ride a bike, jog, lift weights, stretch—whatever fits into your busy schedule. Marian varies her routine daily to prevent boredom, even though she felt overwhelmed by everything at first. However, she decided that her schedule was *never* too busy to take the stairs instead of the escalator or to take the extra lap at the mall, most women's other favorite form of "exercise" (just like Lori). Marian also nearly learned the hard way that swiping the credit card is not a form of "exercise." Her emotional stress was one thing, but her financial stress was something that she could absolutely not "afford" right now. She returned all of her impulse purchases, which nearly maxed out her cards, and gave all of her credit cards except one to her sister for safekeeping. She decided to spend all of exercise time at the gym and not at the mall. Smart gal! Marian recommends 45 minutes a day of exercise, although most of the fitness gurus say 30 minutes. No way could she do just 30 minutes and maintain her daily sweet tooth fix; 45 minutes are the recommended daily dose for her and her fellow menopausal sugar addicts. The more Marian exercised, the more weight she lost. "Now if only I could get the weight loss to affect all of the *right* areas on my body," she said to me. And what female would not agree with that? The weight redistribution never goes where we would like it to go, does it? Marian took up the most aggressive form of exercise that she could think of: kickboxing. You can just imagine what person she focused on as she kicked her way into physical shape. Marian is now pursuing a certificate to become a kickboxing teacher. She has met some amazing women in her classes who happen to have amazing single brothers. It just keeps getting better for her.

Our California girl, Joan, gets up really early and puts in her time before work. We all know how hard it is to rise and shine at 5:30 a.m., but the early wake-up provides a great jumpstart to her day. The newest research in a leading women's magazine says that exercising on an empty stomach is better for you because it forces your body to burn fat, so since she hadn't been sleeping well anyway, Joan decided to get up and make a more productive use of her time. (Punching the pillow does *not* count as productive use of your exercise time. Or maybe it does, depending on your point of view; it's a little like boxing in a way, I think). This early morning workout also gives her the time to think, meditate, and pray. For Joan it has become a great time to say thank you for all of the things that she *does* have in her life. She now leaves the house with those raised endorphin levels carrying her through her workday. It also helps her smile more and gives her a break from crying. This past spring she completed her first half-marathon; her smiling, adoring new beau was waiting for her at the finish line with a dozen roses. Wow.

Erica, an age 30+ college student divorcee and the youngest member by far in our group, walks every day at lunch, no matter the weather. Just that 15 minutes or more helps her avoid coming down with the two o'clock carbo crash, when her eyes would droop and cross from her lack of sleep. She used to wish every day for a 20-minute catnap. Sorry we are not in Mexico or at summer camp: no siestas or quiet time for American adults. Erica eventually extended her walk time and now walks just about everywhere. She recently adopted a mutt from the pound, and they are inseparable. Soon to begin agility training, they plan to tour the U.S. entering agility competitions, enjoying each other's company, as Erica prefers her dog's company to any male that she has met recently.

The Feisty Woman's Guide to Surviving Mr. Wonderful

Kim, who seemed like a lifelong acquaintance, began to take a stroll with her neighbors after dinner. Now that is a great way to end anyone's day. She and her friends have a good laugh with each other and enjoy the beautiful sunsets, one of the advantages of living in the country atop a mini-mountain. When her neighbors are not at home or are busy, she still goes out, but puts the cell phone into overdrive and chats with friends as she walks. The walking seems to go more quickly for Kim, even if her friends on the cell ask what that gasping in her voice is all about. She tells me that she just lies and tells her friends that it must be the bad reception from the country. We both know that cell phone reception can cover up those tears that seem to pop up at the worst moments. Or tell them the truth. Good friends always understand. Kim and her neighbors all joined the gym together and are taking spinning, yoga, and dance classes there, all the while checking out the healthy-looking male patrons.

The fitness freak of our group, Fran, decided to try yoga, which opened up totally new avenues of exercising for her. Not only is the stretching great, but she also discovered that the food at one area yoga spa was to die for. She never knew that healthy food could taste so good. And the quiet time at meals was a new way for her to enjoy food. She generally *never* ate in silence, but once she tried it she decided that the food *did* taste better. Now Fran visits a spa at least twice a year to treat herself. The massages, therapeutic healing, and personal guidance sessions have been a real bonus for her body and soul alike. Fran always comes back totally refreshed and renewed. She decided that she needed this pampering more than ever during this time in her life. Her next goal is tai chi, which she hopes to be able to continue practicing as long as some of the 90-year-olds in her class. All of this fit living has helped her as she now is fighting breast cancer.

One suggestion that may or may not work for you was contributed by a male friend who was going through the same sort of recovery period as some of my female friends: go fishing! Apparently sitting all by yourself by the water, in the quiet, can clear your mind and help you work things through. Just remember the bug spray: nothing like a pesky mosquito to break the silence. It doesn't matter if you don't catch anything; who wants to clean it anyway? This gent always took along some cold ones on the really hot days, which might help in more ways than one. This also counts as exercise as you walk to and from the fishing hole or row your rented boat to and from he middle of the lake: you're sure to forget one or two items so that you will have to make multiple trips to the car. Never underestimate the power of nature. This man has since remarried and has three children.

Are you a water baby? Our fellow exerciser Pam is. "Just think of water," she says. No, it doesn't always mean a trip to the bathroom, but it could involve a bubble bath, a long warm shower, or a cool drink. She recommends drinking at least half your weight in ounces. So if you weigh 130, that means that you should drink 65 ounces a day—about 2 quarts. A swim might also help. "When I swim laps," Pam says, "somehow the water washes everything away." Feeling free and new every time she came up out of the water, Pam swam those laps and watched as she slimmed down and became totally fit. She plans to keep swimming until she feels comfortable enough to shed her clothes at a nude beach and swim totally naked in the water, just like a newborn babe.

Do you remember the time when McDonald's was giving out free pedometers? I still have mine. However, I decided to get myself a more high tech model, one that I could not cheat with. I recently started doing the 5,000 steps per day challenge. I challenged two fellow teacher walking pals to do the same. These two women are just like me: really competitive. We were constantly comparing our "step-page" at every turn, even while we cut back on the fries at McDonald's, instead switching to the healthier salads. Amazing how much walking you do in a day as a teacher. We were really proud of ourselves when that 10,000 mark appeared on our pedometers. We improved our overall health and well being, setting a positive example for our students. Walking is probably the oldest and simplest form of exercise. A half-hour at least three or four days a week will help reduce inflammation and ease the pain of arthritis, according to many doctors and health experts. I felt better just reading this and now it is part of my daily routine.

Diamond

Exercise can help you walk away from your hurt and toward a healthier you. It's hard to cry when you are walking at a face pace. You can run, too. Running away from life may seem like a great idea, but it doesn't work because you end up right back at home anyway. Choose your own exercise program and embrace it.

Chapter 7

Your Nutritional Health . . . Not Your Mental Health

(That chapter comes later in the book)

God knows that you feel pretty crappy right now. You feel blah, washed out, and downright ornery. Every pore seems to hurt; even your teeth ache. Could this be connected to all that crying you've been doing? Enough already. Time to get it together in this area of your life. Time to feel better and take care of yourself. Time to eat! Almost every woman I know is a great consumer of food, and (except for me) enjoys cooking. Time to get out those pots and pans and pamper your palette. The women of this chapter are all avid cooks, some gourmet, some not. I fit into the latter category.

As a former student of mine named Barbara always said so well, "Perhaps so." Food kept her going through the day and helped bolster her through the early rough patch of her breakup with her college boyfriend. She needed the fuel to keep on going. After the initial shock of her Mr.

Wonderful's actions, she didn't eat for three days, in part because she was too busy crying. Luckily, her college friends were returning from their break and happened to stop by, and they wound up feeding her. Food had absolutely no appeal for her at that point; just standing up was about all she could do between prolonged periods of weeping and wailing. Hunger didn't bother her at all; she really believed that she was in shock—and who wouldn't be? Not even that favorite of all female foods, chocolate, had any appeal to her. This was a total perversion of her being, since she had always considered chocolate to be a major food group—as all feisty ladies, young and old, do.

The person she saw in the mirror looked like no one that she even knew. She wondered how in the world she could keep on going. Her life truly sucked at this point. But after numerous conversations with family and friends who urged her to eat, she finally did and she did it for herself. "From now on," she said, "things need to be done by and for me and no one else." It was a scary, yet totally calming feeling for her. At least now she knew why things had been so weird and out of sorts in her life. And she then knew that she would make it to the other side of this disaster. It was time to take care of herself: what a liberating feeling that was for her, the total caregiver for everyone but herself. And cook she did. Barbara took every cooking class that she could, updated her apartment kitchen, and now is known as a superb, healthy, college student/ gourmet cook. She is creating a cookbook for the recently unattached college woman that is filled with healthy recipes—and yes, even the decadent chocolate desserts are pretty healthful. What a great cookbook that will be; I plan to buy one for myself.

I read in one of my women's magazines that so many women overeat during their initial breakup phase; others do not eat at all. One woman mentioned in another article named Julie had gone for three days without any food and desperately needed to eat something. (Seems that this extreme happens with more women than I ever thought). Strangely enough, chocolate was not her first choice, preferring a salad with grilled chicken. For Julie, all of those healthy eating habits really came through when she needed them. She had been trained by the best (herself) and gradually ate one meal, then two meals a day. Three were impossible then, and even now she often skips dinner. She has learned to eat only when she is hungry and until she is full; no stuffing needed. She listened to her body and followed its lead; since her head was in the clouds and wasn't really working anyway, she thought she'd be better off to follow her stomach. She continues to eat like this today. "I am 15 pounds lighter," she says, "and trimmer than ever." Julie even rewarded herself by getting a new wardrobe, a suggestion offered in an earlier chapter. She realized that it was finally all about her and what she needed. Lucky gal. She married a chef and still eats healthfully, instilling her eating habits in her children.

Even if you don't feel like cooking, something that I have always hated anyway, schedule a meal out with friends or join a meal/movie club. I took along another female friend just to be safe. While you eat you discuss the movie plot, actors, scenery, etc. You can just eat and listen or join in the discussion. Mostly I just listened and enjoyed being around well-spoken, semi-intelligent people. You can probably use the company because being alone in the house after all these years is still hard (although it does get easier). You can also take the leftovers home for lunch the next day, an added bonus.

Seems also that every health practitioner has advice for you, too. My nutritionist, Dr. Marylin, offered guidance, patience, kind words, and supplements that helped me a lot during this stressful, painful time. Drinking melatonin really does help you sleep. De-stress tonics are best taken in huge amounts. Vitamins help keep you going, especially when taken with . . . dark chocolate. Best of all, she said, "You will survive this because women are strong, resilient, and hardy beings. We are much tougher than men, anyway."

In her office among the many journals filled with alternative medicines, techniques, and traditional remedies that were proven to work was an article on cough therapy. As previously mentioned and as strange as it sounds, this was one of the more unusual things that worked for me—but then this is also an unusual time for me. It was explained in the article in this way: just cough and cough and cough and cough some more. It gets all traces of his being out of your system. Don't laugh; just try it. You will feel lighter, freer, and less stressed. I have allergies and cough a lot anyway, so why not focus the coughing to benefit me? Whenever I hear someone coughing a lot, now, I always wonder. Maybe she has read this article, too.

While getting through one day at a time, my nurse neighbor, Doris, felt her clothing fitting more loosely and started to weigh in daily to find out what was going on. She had started to lose weight and was feeling more comfortable in her clothing, which had started to hang on her medium frame. When she did weigh herself, she was pleasantly surprised that she had lost weight, but also at the amount that she had lost. What a way to lose weight? "My luck," she said. "I start to get thinner, but at what expense? Sometimes life just sucks."

As she started to eat again, she felt better and her weight got back to a normal level. She was still on base according to the weight charts, so she wasn't worried because at least she wasn't overeating for a change. To this day, she continues to weigh the same, but emotionally feels 100 percent better. "What a great way to get your weight and eating under control," she said, smiling all the way to a smaller dress size.

Every health-conscious Web site stresses the need to drink plenty of water in the best of times. But when you are crying so much, you also need to replace all the fluids that you are losing. It also keeps you moving, even if only to the bathroom. A kindergarten teacher that I met in the nutritionist's office, Harrie, had an interesting experience with this. Apparently her classroom had its own adjoining bathroom. Her little ones were always in there and so was she. One day one of them remarked, "Señora, why are you always in here with me? I do not need your help. I need my privacy, too." Harrie took that advice and reduced her water intake. Too much of a good thing isn't good either, as she discovered. Out of the mouths of babes.

If you have any food allergies, they really seem to crop up during this time of turmoil in your life. A California teacher friend named Angelina broke out in hives whenever her Mr. Wonderful's name came up in conversation. She also developed more rashes in the course of their separation than she could have ever imagined. Guess that stress comes out in many forms. Her dermatologist questioned her about her life and what was wigging her out. Even he suggested that she "dump the fat bastard" which she was planning to do anyway. Surprise—once they separated, the rashes subsided and clearer skin prevailed. Another benefit as you shed Mr. Wonderful from your life.

Diamond

Just remember, the most important words of food wisdom for feisty women everywhere are these: always remember to eat. You will not survive physically and emotionally without food. Eat whatever you want, really. *Just eat.* Your health truly will suffer at first if you do not eat, and food keeps you going as you plot your life course without Mr. Wonderful. Food is every woman's friend, always was and always will be.

Chapter 8

Home Improvements Will Brighten Your Outlook

Coming home to the place that I'd shared with Mr. Wonderful was totally depressing in those first weeks I spent alone. I thought that I smelled his cologne when I opened my front door. Since I physically removed him I had to remove all traces of him, too. We all know that scents can be a powerful entity and the sooner they're gone the better. This was an extremely painful part of recovery, but one that today feels totally peaceful and right.

Start with whatever room you want, and enlist the help of as many female friends as you can. They can be with you in person or in spirit, by phone or through e-mailing their suggestions to you. My friend since elementary school, Deb, decided she would pay me a long overdue visit and help me through my muddle. We decided that the bedroom needed to be done first. Since my ex always considered himself master of the bedroom (and what male doesn't), she suggested that we start there: Salvation Army to the rescue.

We packed up all of the sheets, towels, and bedding that he had ever touched. We also sliced and diced our fair share too, as it helped me get out my anger, all the while playing Gloria Gaynor's "I Will Survive". New curtains and shades helped a lot, even though I did better on gloomy days than sunny ones at first because of my distressed mood. We had someone paint the bathroom to remove his smell, which would not disappear no matter what. While sitting in his closet and talking about how my life had changed, we left it vacant for months. We knew that I would fill it when I was ready—which was sooner than I ever thought. Deb suggested that we take the scissors to a fair amount of his remaining clothing, but most of it was donated to a local church thrift shop in the hopes that someone he totally disliked would have the chance to use them. He had no empathy for those less fortunate than him. And I got the tax credit. Sometimes, the world does get it right. Thanks for all of your help, Deb.

Next I called in another neighbor, Melissa, to help me continue this makeover. Unfortunately, she was in the same boat as me. Her husband of 11+ years decided that he could do better elsewhere and bought a new house for his new love interest, with their money. We agreed to help each other through the house "makeover" project (I later returned the favor and helped her in her home redo). The upstairs spare bedroom/study was always his messy, disorganized, and extremely cluttered domain. Melissa and I could finally see the floor, clear the dust, open the windows without fear of papers flying everywhere, and set up a workshop for yours truly. I was no longer relegated to a small corner in the bedroom for my office space. Melissa organized the bookshelves and storage space for the first time in nearly ten years, so that I could get and keep myself better organized. In my state of mind, I needed to have everything in a certain place or I would never find it. More brain fog, I guess.

Next I headed down to the living room as I decided to keep on updating and rearranging things to move him out of my life. I single-handedly kept the local economy thriving with my purchases of furniture, lamps, slipcovers, and the like. I needed a new look for my home and I wholeheartedly dove into the project. While power tools and I are a dangerous mix, I was fortunate enough to have friends who could assist me with this project. They were a Godsend. I was already coping with a wounded spirit, so I surely didn't need bodily injuries too. Enough pain already!

And then Martha Stewart came into my life. Seeing her on TV gave me new ideas for redecorating. That she had served time for the same crime for which many men received a mere slap on the wrist endeared her to me even more. She kept her cool and has prevailed despite her shoddy treatment in the media and in the courts. Although my new digs felt warm and cozy, cool fall breezes kept the place really chilly. Martha's stylish new curtains helped somewhat, but still I felt cold as I sat on the couch. Sitting alone may have had something to do with the big chill in my house, but I also recalled that Mr. Wonderful had often discussed our need to replace the old, faded, leaky glass patio door. Like many things we needed, he just never got around to it, so I took charge, bought a new door and had it installed. The addition of that sliding door glass changed my whole view of the outside world. The clean glass and shiny windows brought a new "light" into my home. The repainted living room took on a new glow. The throw pillows, blankets, and coffee mugs (all recommended by my new friend Martha) added to the ambience. Peace, brightness, and calmness replaced the negativity, sarcasm, gloom and doom that I had endured for so long. More light goes a long way, baby, to lifting the spirits. Guess that research I'd read on light and mood really was true. I am sure that Martha had read it, too.

The most dreaded room in the house was next on my agenda: the kitchen. Diane, another elementary school colleague, rescued me from this often cleaned, but never used, room. Funny that we both have never liked to cook and that we both had to makes strides in this direction. While we were left with cupboards as bare as Old Mother Hubbard's—gives away my age, I'm afraid—Diane and I proceeded to eat out as much as we could. More support for the economy, we thought. Still, with a new top-of-the-line stove, (the only large home purchase he ever made), we both began to try to cook at my home. Pity that the pots and pans were gone as well (to be returned six months later, after 16 emails asking for them). After many failed attempts we did succeed in making omelets. We ate so many eggs that we felt like scratching at the ground whenever we were outside. Both of us rarely eat eggs today and then only when we eat out: maybe too many bad memories.

Chicken was next on my menu. Salads were easy because they came ready made in a bag. Soup? Empty the can and nuke. And so the cooking journey continues, a topic for another book. Yes, Diane and I both miss our respective Mr. Wonderful's cooking, but honestly, *that's about it.* And for the record, we were not as bad in the kitchen as we were led to believe. Another myth bites the dust. We may not be gourmet cooks, but we have the confidence to tackle almost any type of cooking.

The bathroom in my home was next and over time it became a true masterpiece. It was painted, trimmed, "rebathed and reshowered, and refloored". New wall decor made it one room that reflected my sense of style and cleanliness. My Mr. Wonderful would never clean a bathroom, no matter how bad it got, but imagine how I felt cleaning this room—and him—out of my life in one shot. Wow. What a great day that was.

My neighbor Lisa kept bringing me stories of other home makeover projects that she had read about. One was especially priceless. A woman she knew came home from work some days after her divorce to find that all the furniture was gone. As she burst into tears walking through her totally empty house, she marveled at the absence of one item that he never seemed to use correctly, the toilet seat. He never put it down anyway, but now he needed it?

In spring, my garden really needed some attention. All those years that he focused on growing vegetables that were feed for the slugs and only produced monster cucumbers had come to an end. Shrubs and sunflowers replaced the unsuccessful vegetable medley. Flowers in the front garden are now as colorful as ever with a variety, quantity, and bloom never before witnessed in my development. "Oohs and aahs" resound whenever neighbors walk by. Seems that I am blessed with a green thumb and am enjoying playing in the dirt.

Diamond

Your home will become a cozy, comfortable environment free from Mr. Wonderful, aka Mr. Stress, and an oasis for you eventually. Just give it time. It also will look like you again. And that's not so bad at all. Out with the old and in with the new really does work.

Section 3:

Revival Time for Your Brain

Psychologists say that stress reduces your mental acuity by half—explaining why you can never find your car keys when you're late—and that extreme stress reduces it extremely. Now's the time to de-stress and get those synapses firing again.

Chapter 9

Re-Intellectualizing and Unfreezing Your Brain Cells

Although you seem to be hurting all over, give your mind something new to focus on. Your brain needs that new focus to help you move on with your life. I decided that studying might be better for me than crying, so I gave it a try. Being the high school valedictorian came with certain expectations. I always considered myself to be a top-notch student, and given the brain fog that I had felt during my gut-wrenching divorce, I eventually knew that I had had enough of the self-help books I'd been reading.

I started attending a women's book club at the local library, and have included their stories in this chapter. After getting acquainted, it seemed that we were all intelligent women who had survived the loss of a life partner or spouse or were divorced. We helped each other in so many ways that I cannot even list them all here. What a special group of feisty women.

For a change of pace, the women in my group rejected some of the library book club suggestions and came up with a book list of our own. Susan started reading biographies, which offered her some tips that others had used in their struggles to improve their life status. "Their words," Abby quickly agreed, "just might give us hope, insight, and a chuckle as we read how other women have coped in their various stages of life as a couple or non-couple." "Just check out the *New York Times* bestseller list," added Mary. "Some famous or infamous person is usually dishing about their life struggles and triumphs." Susan suggested, however, that we all avoid the mushy ones. "Some of us are not ready for a happy ending," she said, "especially when your happy ending was taken from you." Her husband had recently passed. What a wise woman; every recently widowed or about-to-be-divorced woman was nodding in agreement. Finally, we also decided that it was better to read a real life story in a book than have to read about some "wanna-be" you might have heard of in the *Globe* or the *Star. We were all set.*

Donna also joined our book club but at first rarely joined in our discussions. Our Monday night group was a great mix of funny, strong, dynamic, feisty, menopausal women. We could never keep the room cool enough it seemed. Sometimes it was hard to believe that we all had read the same book, but alas, we had. We all disliked the weak, noncommittal men who either had affairs or abandoned their wives to find themselves. We all clapped for and nodded in agreement about the strong, vital women who persevered despite seemingly insurmountable odds. Donna finally spoke up one night when we were choosing our book for the following month. She drew the line only when she thought that we kept reading books from the authors of a certain country (Spain) that she did not want to hear anything about. She had to take a break from anything to do with the Spanish and their love of cheating attitude exemplified by her ex-partner. But after dropping out briefly, she missed the camaraderie that she felt with us and returned to our ranks after a short break. We too had missed her sarcastic wit and funny, if off-topic, comments.

While the book club occupied my Monday nights, I found that I might need other ways to stretch my brain. As a musician, I also felt that I needed to keep learning new techniques to improve my teaching and to expand my learning. I found steel drumming fit that need perfectly. I used drumming to relieve stress (add a certain face to the drum head and pound away), and to learn about multicultural music. I continue drumming today and have added steel drums to my repertoire of musical instruments. Every summer I attend a top-notch university that has a summer program for novice and developing steel drummers. I no longer visualize anyone's face on the drums, but now focus on the joy of drumming, which is found to be therapeutic and celebratory in many cultures, my own included.

The mystery book addict in our book group, Sherry, decided to learn to curse in sign language. All of the curse words imaginable were taught in her first ASL (American Sign Language) class at a local community college and were frequently reviewed throughout the semester; seemed that other book club members wanted to know those words, too. We learned a few words every week; I can still curse fluently in ASL as can many of my fellow book club members. After two semesters of study, Sherry became a great "signer" and has been a translator at a few public events in her town. About six months into her new job, she witnessed a couple arguing in the mall. When familiar vulgar sign language caught her eye, she responded in kind to the woman signing. They both had a great laugh at the expense of another Mr. Wonderful. The two women shared coffee and a good laugh that afternoon and remain friends today. Sometimes it really is better to keep your comments to yourself, but what a great way to get it out of your system and to curse in a language that only about five percent of the population understands.

Linda, the leader of our group, renamed us the "Monday Menopausers" because of our room temperature issues, quirky comments, and odd interest in cursing. She took Sherry's sign language classes a step further. Since she really enjoyed foreign language classes in high school and college—the one place where she finally started to understand the foibles and insane rules of the English language—she decided that maybe some language therapy might help her. As her world was also changing, she listed her top five or six curse words and set out to learn them in as many languages as possible. When she got truly angry and frustrated with her life status, she discovered that cursing in any language requires a forceful tone, certain body stances, facial gestures, and true guts to say what you are thinking—even though most people will not understand what you are saying. She studied Spanish, German, a Native American dialect, Welsh, Hawaiian, and any other language that anyone she knew spoke. And she vowed to learn to curse fluently in all of them. At first her friends' responses were curious. After she explained her separated/divorcing situation, they each smiled and gave her the words that she needed to get it all out of her system. Now she can "let 'er rip" in an assortment of languages and gestures appropriate for any social setting. What a feeling of power. While this may not seem intellectual to some readers, it did require considerable mental stamina to keep all of these words straight in her sometimes scrambled brain. Today she is proud that she can still curse in a number of languages, but finds fewer opportunities to employ this plethora of knowledge. She has moved on from her own Mr. Wonderful and is happy and content. If, however, the urge or need ever did arise, I am sure that she could easily retrieve those words.

We "Monday Menopausers" also discussed our need to join the age of technology. As someone who grew up in the '70s, Karen had resisted the technology of the new millennium for a long time, just as most of the "Menopausers" had. As soon as we all learned one computer program and mastered it, a new version came out and our mastery skills seemed to have gone for nothing. While she still may consider herself to be a technological troglodyte, Karen now writes daily on her laptop, checks her email on her new iPhone, and uses only one remote for her TV, DVD/CD player and other devices. I know that she may have disappointed all of her hippie friends who still scorn the use of technology, but she has moved on and so have most of them too, I am sure. She knew that she joined the techie parade when she bought a laptop bag and could fill it with all of her gizmos and gadgets. She still has her daily computer struggles, some of which are caused by glitches within the computer and not by her. She began taking classes and brought some of her questions to our group.

Sure enough we had some computer experts in our group who offered her help in her techie struggles. You can now follow her on Facebook and Twitter.

Karen was not the only one in our group to struggle with technology. I have faced my own techie challenges while writing this book. Even though I hired a Web designer, I struggled with what exactly to add to the Web site. My Twitter posts started slowly but have since improved. I still struggled with Facebook, but have decided that I need to get with the times and be a part of the technology scene. Wish me luck; I will need it. And by the way, our book club continues to meet on Mondays. We are searching for a new name.

Diamond

Keep your mind busy and active. It will let you know when you can slow down, settle down, and deal with all of the hurt and pain that you are feeling. It will also guide you as you develop new pursuits and interests just waiting for you out in the world.

Chapter 10

Your Job, Your Godsend

We all know that work is an important part of life, especially for teachers. The staff room provides more information, suggestions, and updates on politics, religion, sex, and gossip than any Internet connection or magazine that you encounter at the grocery checkout. At the very least our jobs pay the bills, but are also a big part of who we are. The staff room support really kept me going through the rough times and provided an oasis from the hurt, pain, and sorrow that I felt in my home. Other friends have felt just the opposite; they recovered better at home.

All the stories from women in this chapter come from staff room conversations and sharing. The names have been changed to protect the innocent and not so innocent.

My fellow senior teacher Susan, in the same situation as I was, spent her time focusing intently on her job. Her mind needed to be occupied as much as it could be with projects that did not involve her soon to be ex-Mr. Wonderful husband of 30 years. However, she was not as focused as she always had been, so she started to keep a list of what she needed to do and of what she had done each day. Before this note taking started, one Monday morning she got dressed for work, went to get in the car, and noticed that she felt really chilly. She had been taking one of the more commonly prescribed antidepressant medications, which had created more fog for her than she already had. She was wearing her long sweater, but not her pants. From that day on, Susan checked off each job on her list so that she felt that she was at least accomplishing something on the professional front because her life on the personal front (except for now being properly clothed at all times) truly sucked at the moment. Susan also started feeding her medication to her plants and did they ever grow. She kept a small notebook for list making and snipped the corner of the page as she completed all of projects on that page. It felt good that she was accomplishing something in at least one part of her life. Her notebook-snipping idea has been used by many of my other friends as we have gotten older and needed organizational help in our lives.

Norma decided to take on a few extra projects at work to keep her sanity and her mind occupied during her divorce. She remained on her many committees and honored all previous work commitments—even if her Mr. Wonderful could not honor his commitment to her. (Sorry, I just had to get that crack in for her sake, words we heard her utter often). Norma needed the structure and familiarity to keep her afloat right now. She attended all the work meetings that she could (most of us dreaded them) and volunteered for any committee that she could, even if she felt like crying—which she did on the way to many of them. She always arrived early in case the tears started and she needed time to recover before she entered any meeting. "Arriving with red eyes and a red nose will only embarrass me," she always said, "but it really does make the others a bit kinder toward me. The only bonus is that no one will speak to you about your appearance; only are a true friend would do that. Most of them do not know what to say, however, even though a simple "I'm sorry" would do". Norma still remains an integral part of the school and is happily "Mr. Wonderful" free.

Joan recommended that if you do have to cry, leave before you need to use that humongous wad of tissues. Nothing brings more attention to you than a big honk from clearing your nose; if they didn't notice you before, they will now. She often arrived late to meetings and left early; we all understood. Eventually she passed out tissues to others in need, borrowing from her stash in the hall storage closet. All the students in school knew who had the soft tissues and often descended on her as well.

Donna served on at least four committees at school and developed a side business as an event planner. We all felt that was a perfect fit for her over-the-top planning skills and love of meetings. Her new husband would give her the sun and the moon if he could; he told her that he was attracted to her because of her kindness, compassion, and good looks. What a mensch. We all hoped that he had brothers for all of us, but he had only sisters.

Annette confided her impending divorce story to one friend in her work group whom she knew she could trust. Soon her whole team and lunch group became her support system. They took her out to eat, to the movies and concerts, and supported her through her divorce. She knew that she could count on them with her life when she was sequestered on the jury of a murder trial for six weeks. It was a harrowing experience for her, especially when the convicted murderer swore revenge on the entire jury. Today, Annette remains safe, happy, and loved with her family and new husband, who just happened to be a police officer. She also helps run a divorce support group for minority women.

Lou Ann decided that she was no longer taking any kind of bunk from incompetent, mean, obnoxious, people, including her soon to be ex-husband. She vowed to assert herself tactfully in all situations from now on. This took a bit of energy because she felt like letting these people have it many times, but tact won out in the end. She simply let them implode and then calmly stated her case. Lou Ann's reaction made them feel even worse about their behavior than she ever could have imagined. Most of them knew "through the school grapevine" about what she was enduring at the moment. (The school pipeline is better than any gossip rag as a news source). Her calm, cool, collected demeanor surprised everyone and made them think twice about their attitude and behavior. If she could remain calm and in control through her personal struggles, they certainly should be able to as well, since they all live with a beautiful wife/handsome husband, 2.2 children, and golden retriever, secure in their gated communities. (Just a small bit of pent-up jealousy there from Lou Ann). She went on to become an outstanding school guidance counselor to both students and staff alike. Lou Ann is now on the school conflict resolution team.

Since work is all-important during this phase, be sure to get as much sleep as you can so that you'll be at your best.

Fred always needed to be focused and have as clear a head as he could at school, especially because he was teaching middle students. His job was one of the few constants in his life, so he did his best to keep it that way. When his fiancée canceled their wedding two weeks before it was scheduled, he was totally flummoxed. He took melatonin to sleep if he had to, but avoided sleep-inducing drugs if at all possible. The less mental fog, as some do feel even from taking melatonin, the better. When he still had problems with sleep and encountered really awful nightmares, Fred purchased a dream catcher or two or three and hung them everywhere he could around his bed. A Native American healing tool consisting of a willow hoop with an imitation spider web made of yarn, the dream catcher helped him feel that it would "catch" and filter out his bad dreams and allow only good thoughts to enter his mind. According to tradition, once the sun came up, all his bad dreams would disappear. It seemed to work, because his sleep was calmer and less disturbed (good choice of words, given his feelings toward his ex). He also purchased a chiropractic pillow (to help with the real or imagined pain in his neck). Seems that the non-drug remedies worked best for him. I guess he was just a more natural man than any of us ever thought. Who knew?

Luckily for all of us at school, he used his wedding hall reservation to host the holiday staff party. What a great party that was (The holiday party actually continued at that venue for many years). He also used the plane tickets from his canceled honeymoon trip to travel to visit his ancestral home in Europe. He found relatives that he never knew he had. They had a blast and some of them became his holiday travel pals. They are now nearly arrested wherever they go, but remain free to enjoy life to the fullest. Fred has since become engaged again and the school holiday party location (former wedding reception hall venue) has been changed, much to the dismay of his fellow staff members. Still, they are happy for Fred and his new fiancée.

Heidi originally kept all work-related and professional phone numbers written on little pieces of paper that she started losing no matter how hard she tried not to. She added them to her cell phone but now she had to remember not to lose her cell phone. Unfortunately, Heidi did this once and had a major panic attack until she finally found it. She now places the phone in the same place everyday and vows that this will not happen again. It resides in the school safe along with the phones of all staff members going through separations, divorces, and un-engagements. Things like phone numbers, names, email address, and the like were simply too hard to remember in her present condition. She also stores car keys, handbags, and other disappearing items for staff members in the safe. This way everyone can leave work with all of their personal items as they depart through the office area. All unclaimed items left in the safe are donated to charity at the end of every school year. You would be surprised how many items are donated every year.

Diamond

Work will be your lifesaver for a long time, believe me. And when you can't wait to go home, you know that you are on your way to resuming your life.

Chapter 11

It Might Be Time to Become a Legal Eagle

Once it has really hit you about the infidelities of Mr. Wonderful (even though he swears that this was the only one—right), you should first check out all your legal, financial, and other personal records. Needless to say, they are probably strewn everywhere around the house since organization was not one of his virtues (were there any?). This will be a really tough job even though you finally know why he was so distant, behaving so weirdly, etc. It also explains the long hours at work (right), the weekends of working (right again), and those repeated trips here and obviously there (right once again). You also know why he did not want to go to counseling with you, even though now you realize that you should have gone all by yourself. Oh, well, better late to the counselor than never.

Back in chapter 4, I discussed some of the potential legal perils of taking revenge. But now it's time to remind you that you need to protect yourself legally in other ways.

(I should also remind you to read the disclaimer at the beginning of this book.) I am including stories from stay-at-home mom friends who are dismissed by many folks for not "working" outside the home. These ladies give a new meaning to the word feisty. I'll follow these with tales from my cohabitating friends.

First and foremost, call your lawyer and do not rely on the rulings that you watch on *Judge Judy*. Debbie, a fortysomething stay-at-home mom, was a Judge Judy junkie, getting all of her legal advice from that show. Wrong source, she soon found out. Have a divorce attorney check out all the legalities of as many things as you can, as soon as you can. Debbie learned this the hard way. Her brain and heart were so totally scrambled that she could hardly think, but this call was the most important one she ever made. She gave her lawyer a heads-up about the situation and received advice about just how far you can push things (further than you think). Her soon-to-be-ex-husband told her that his lawyer would take care of everything. Hmmm. Never believe anything that's too good to be true. Fortunately, Debbie and her ex settled things pretty fairly after her divorce lawyer entered the picture.

Sally nearly needed a lawyer before her divorce proceedings officially started. She had just left an especially bitter session with the attorneys and her soon-to-be-ex. As she walked by the ex's brand new sports car, she noticed that it was unlocked. Bags for a weekend getaway were in the back. Not one to resist this opportunity, Sally grabbed a few items and stuffed them in her car just as her Mr. Wonderful approached. Hoping that he could not spot them in her car, she quickly started the car and drove away. Along each rest stop on the I-95 corridor she tossed away one of his items right next to a trash bin. She laughed to herself when she imagined her ex-Mr. Wonderful opening his half-empty bag and finding no pants, toiletries, or socks for the weekend. Sally is hoping that some lucky person might still be enjoying a few of those "Sally-bought" items today. No charges were ever filed.

Barbara was always belittled by her Mr. Wonderful, who totally underestimated her and her resourcefulness. He considered her stay-at-home Mom status beneath him and his high-powered business friends. Barbara took matters into her own hands when he started being late for dinner, having meetings, and all the usual dodges. She decided to call their financial planner. She had her soon-to-be ex's name removed from all of her accounts (from her pre-at home days) that might have benefited him in any way. And she left her name on his accounts, not mentioning her changes in the process. She remained his insurance beneficiary for six months after they were separated. What a guy. She kept as many household bills in his name as long as long as she could. "He at least owes me that," Barbara said. Right. He proceeded to drop her from the auto insurance without her consent, canceled the utility service (a law breaker), and changed the locks on all of the doors. When she arrived with the sheriff, her ex had a big "change" in his tune and promptly reinstated the car insurance and utility service, and had the old locks reinstalled. Even though she helped him build a business, she did kiss that investment goodbye. Barbara quietly got her shares out of the company with the help of her office mole. Those benefits did not go to wife number #4. Barbara also got half of his pension in her divorce settlement and his social security benefits when he passed.

And now to the legal issues of my unmarried, cohabitating friends. After ten not-so-blissful years, Carol and her Mr. Wonderful were separating. While never married, they were the beneficiaries on each other's wills. She promptly removed his name from her will. And decided that if he forgot to remove her name, tough. Wouldn't that be some payback? Carol had already checked the common law information just to be sure that he was entitled to nothing in her, not his, home. That law remains in effect in only three states in the U.S. and not any state in its right mind. After nearly ten years together, Carol could still count on the fingers of one hand the things that he had bought for their home. She checked the law out more than once for her own peace of mind. Still, he pleaded for all the items that he had bought. Carol decided not to give him one more thing than those items even when he told her that he was living in his car. "Should have thought about that sooner," she says. Her home remains her own oasis and cozier than ever.

Kerry told her Mr. Wonderful to move out ASAP, the sooner the better for both of them. She watched him pack as much as she could handle. It hurt like hell, she says, but it took six months and 16 e-mails and a lawyer to have him return all of her things he "accidentally" packed, that upon return were still packed in their original boxes. They were dated and numbered, the first things that he ever packed. Kerry also "helped" him pack by searching through his things one final time. Some of his things that she found were disturbing to say the least. Then she knew that his leaving was the best. "He had kept pictures of previous female conquests," she said, "their letters, and some of their possessions, and he took all of my letters to him and pictures of us as well." Weird, huh?

Joanne changed all of the locks before he left. As he packed she decided that he had to come and go on her terms. Some control in this situation made her feel a little bit better. He then knew that she was serious about his leaving, even more so when she informed him that she would not be interested in having dinner with him a few times a week before he left. Joanne found that request totally odd. At that point he was having second thoughts—but she did not.

Put the local police number on your cell phone. Margaret did it just in case things went awry. Many years later she still has it there. Anger and rage are powerful emotions that should never be dismissed or taken lightly. People can do awful things during emotional times. Because he had a temper, Margaret thought he could "snap" at any time and she wanted to be better safe than sorry. One of her friends was choked by her soon-to-be-ex and needed police help fast. Thanks goodness the number was close by when things went sour.

Most of us really don't understand and agree with many facets of the law, but I will add one more comment that my cohabiting friends often heard from their families and friends: "Thank God that you were not married to him. Just imagine how that would have made all of these hassles even worse. Whew. That was a close call." These feisty women trusted their gut about the marriage issue and from now on will always follow that instinct.

Elizabeth Allen

Diamond

By being up on the legalities of your situation, you gain even more control, closure, and confidence in additional decisions that you will need to make. Having the law on your side simply *cannot* hurt!

Section 4:

Food for the Soul

Now that your body and brain are back in something close to working order, it's time to address your soul—and soulfulness—which may have gotten lost in the shuffle.

Chapter 12

Sing and Dance All You Want

We are all aware of the powers of music. As a musician, I know how music can calm, elate, sadden, or excite anyone at any time. Whatever your mood, music can be just the thing to help you out and lift your spirits. Whether you perform music or just listen to it, it may well be the best natural drug that exists—and much cheaper, too. The men and women interviewed for this chapter are all fellow artists and performers in the music field.

Elizabeth, a frequent musical show performer, decided to choose a song as her recovery anthem and play it as many times during the day as she could stand to hear it; when she got the number of repetitions down to a mere six times per day, she knew that she was on the way to letting go of her Mr. Wonderful. Plenty of survival songs have been written and performed over the years. As she asked her friends for suggestions she also listened to a Top 40 station and the latest hit was playing right then and there: Kelly Clarkson to the rescue with "Stronger (What Doesn't Kill You)". She did spend some time listening to Country and Western stations because she believed that the genre specialized in this type of song. But then this type of song has probably been around since the beginning of time, in just about every culture. Elizabeth's research found that Gloria Gaynor's "I Will Survive" was the all-time top choice—great longevity for a song written in the 1970s. Today when she hears this song she boogies along and is surprised how many men and women know all the lyrics. And she also notices how happy they all look when they are performing it. Thanks to the Mr. Wonderfuls of the world for having promoted Gloria to such fame.

Most women and men probably already knew what the #1 choice was, but that may or may not work for you. Kathryn, already a well-established professionally trained singer, channeled Kelly Clarkson in her encore performances of "Stronger (What Doesn't Kill You)" and brought down the house. She sang it in the shower, in the car, everywhere. Kathryn also pretended that she was in a video and acted out this song in her own diva way. Her performances brought smiles, cheers, and plenty of sing-a-longs from fans at her concerts. I, too, would break into song and join in when I heard her sing this one. Singing it, without bursting into tears, let Kathryn know that she had made it through the sadness and could now move on. She lived those words and today is actually thankful that she and her Mr. Wonderful are no longer a couple. "How else would I enjoy performing this song so much," she says, "if I had not lived the words myself?"

Gail a popular local piano teacher exercised to all kinds of music everyday. She often chose music with a good beat for walking, to get her heart rate moving. Armed with one of her many electronic devices, she hit the walking path at a good pace and felt rejuvenated after each exercise sessions. People sometimes stared at her as she was walking and singing, but when they saw the smile on her face they often smiled, too: some even joined her in singing along. At times, calmer, slower tunes did it for her if she felt like crying some more, but more often than not, the "big beat" numbers won out. Moving and music seemed to be a winning combination for Gail. "Try it", she said. "It will work wonders for you."

Studies do show that exercise makes us feel better because of the endorphin release. Add music to that and you have a real winner. Today, Gail can sing along with almost any recovery song while walking and not break into tears, but that did take a while. "So many songs to choose from," says Gail, "and so many trails to conquer." However, she always asks her walking pals to join her only if they are un-phased by some of the looks they may get.

If you are listening to music and feel like crying, just cry. Cindy, a church organist friend, cried at any sentimental song she heard after she separated from her husband of 25 years. "Just might be time for another good one anyway," she said. Since she sat in the balcony to play during worship, no one saw her tears—which was an especially good thing when she played at weddings. Cindy tried to avoid any songs that reminded her of Mr. Wonderful, but that was really difficult. Some songs are so bad that they would make anyone cry, even those women in a better mood than you. "Sometimes it's the song; other times the bad singing really gets to me," said Cindy. We have all been present for that scenario. Gradually she came not to be bothered by those gushy, mushy songs especially when she and one bride shared a knowing smile at wedding rehearsals. Longtime friends, both women had been through a similar breakup and had shared their common misery, but now the bride was truly moving on. Cindy did manage to save one woman from years of misery. The slug of a groom made a pass at Cindy just as the bride was walking up the stairs to the balcony. He never saw his fiancée coming and the wedding was called off.

Kimberly, manager of a local symphony, removed all sentimental songs connected with her Mr. Wonderful from her listening devices. "Hitting the delete key always felt great because I felt that I was deleting one more part of him from my life," she said. This creep had a fling right before their wedding and still wanted to get married even after she found out about his dalliance. Kimberly replaced her old songs with empowering songs, funny songs, and a few kiddie songs. She particularly enjoyed deleting his heavy metal tunes, which she hated anyway (and she could never quite understand the lyrics amid all that guitar thrashing). Her new repertoire of songs reflected her new life, adding long-lost college favorites that held fond memories for her. "If you need any suggestions," she said, "let me know. I can share my list with you." She has one of the most eclectic collections that I have ever heard. I'll just mention the names and let you imagine the song titles: the Stones, Blondie, R.E.M., Bob Marley, Red Hot Chili Peppers, Arcade Fire, Led Zeppelin, Norah Jones, Mozart, Beethoven, Ives, and Gangsta rappers to name a few.

My friend John chose dancing as his music recovery mode. Since he was trained as a modern dancer, he kept up with the best of them on the dance floor. Lots of the most recent pop tunes have a beat that is pretty hard to miss and John grabbed on to that beat and shook his booty, driving some of his blues away. He laughed at himself as he shook, shedding a few pounds in the process. He was truly ready for those TV shows that pair up dancers and wannabe dancers. The dances that had fancy footwork were his specialty. In his state of mind, he had enough to deal with, let alone learning new complicated dance steps, and could have stuck to basics—but he took on the challenge anyway. "Dancing at home," he thought, "might be best at first since I have not been out dancing for a while." So he did practice in the privacy of his home. John knew that he had to avoid any additional public embarrassments at this point since one booty dance revealed more of him than he wanted to. Today, John has a new partner whose dancing is on par with his. What a great way for both of them to enjoy their new life together.

But sometimes, you may need to turn off the music and embrace the silence. Danny, a mid-thirties DJ, just wanted to be alone with his thoughts and emotions, and that was best for his entire being. He had a stressful job and rarely had time to think about his Mr. Wonderful during the workday, which turned out to be a good thing. As he embraced all those quiet times that life has to offer, his own personal music began to play as his recovery continued moving forward. Silence was a large part of it. "It is okay to sit and be still," he said. "The world is such a busy place and we all get wrapped up in the keeping busy part of it, but sometimes just tuning out might be the best way to go. It gives you time to regroup and refocus and rethink all of your recent steps forward in your new life. You might even smile when you realize just how far you have come."

In his silence, Danny started to meditate. New research shows that you can change your familial predisposition for depression by doing daily meditating upon rising in the morning and in the evening. Danny used that technique to move on, to become healthier, and to freak out his mom whenever he visited her. She could never understand how anyone could sit still for 45 minutes and do nothing. Eventually, she left him alone and saved herself a lot of grief. She saved up all her words for him until he was finished meditating and then chatted to her heart's content. Seems the meditating helped him with that, too.

Diamond

Music or the silence: choose that which you need at the moment and save the other for when you may need something different. I could never imagine my life without music, but sometimes the calm, stillness, and peacefulness are better for you. That is the break that you may need from all the cacophony of life. And maybe you will eventually start to sing along with the radio without crying, to hum when taking a walk and rock out at every opportunity as you begin to feel better.

Chapter 13

Get Your Religion Going Again!

As a practicing Christian woman, my experience with Mr. Wonderful profoundly tested that aspect of my life. I knew that I had faith, but what a challenge this was. I asked why God would allow this to be? The answer I got was that we have choices and I had made the wrong one. Let me add that I am not sure if God is a She or a He—or both. Some days I could not figure that one out; others days I was quite sure. And what I thought, and what I feel now will forever be private and way beyond the scope of this book. I have many very religious friends who have been wondering the same things as I have and were more forthright in their thoughts, so let me tell you what they said.

In the trying time after separating from her Mr. Wonderful, Connie tried to get herself to church as often as possible. It had given her so much solace, strength, and support in the past, maybe more so because her husband was the pastor. But he was forced to resign in disgrace after an affair with a church employee, leaving Connie in the lurch. If she felt the need to cry, she just cried, no matter where she was. "God surely understands," she said. And so did the folks in church, even though they stared at her at first. Connie stared back through her tears and saw the care and compassion in their eyes. Many older and even new members passed her a tissue or an entire box whenever she needed it. Everyone in that church had their own sorrow and maybe some had even shared it with her. As she proceeded in her healing, she did remain active in her church, eventually starting one of the city's most popular divorce support groups. Connie's outlook, cooking, and networking gave her time for her own healing. She is now engaged, at the age of 75, to a great guy she met in that support group. What an inspiration she is.

If you are menopausal, full of mood swings, and need a real change in your life, my friend, Sister Diane, can offer some Bible reading suggestions just for you. A former professional musician engaged to be married, one day Dianne sat her fiancée down and informed him that her true calling was the convent. We were all shocked beyond belief. She has since been a nun for more than 25 years and does her fair share of counseling. She recommends two psalms a day. They will fit in perfectly with your mood swings as their content is all over the place, too. They were truly perfect for me. Love, hate, fear, pleading, keeping the faith, losing the faith: it's all there, so check it out.

A wise pastor friend offered counseling to my yoga pal Amy. They discussed the aspects of this challenging time in her life, including her loss of faith, along with many common counseling concerns (most of which began with the word "why"). He let her cry as much as she needed to. As one of the sessions drew to a close, the pastor smiled and asked her what her gut said; she thought that he was crazy and was suddenly talking about digestive issues. She told him that she wasn't sure. He asked her to question her divorce decision once again and wait for the reply. Amy closed her eyes and when it came to her a short time later, she nearly fell out of her seat. This ever so small voice in her gut said that she was on the right course and to keep moving forward with her decision to divorce her husband of ten years. Totally stunned, she felt a strange calmness and sat in total silence for about fifteen minutes, thinking of all of the times that she had ignored this voice.

Amy firmly believes to this day that the little voice that women have—not in their head, not in their heart, but in their gut—is the voice of God guiding you. It was there all along and has been the one that she has been following ever since. "Women sense this more than men," she said, "because we are better listeners and followers of our intuition. They don't call it guy's intuition, now do they?"

Seemed to work for her. She called it her "God-o-meter". To this day, when perplexed about something, Amy still listens, waits, and she might get an answer, but maybe not the one that she expects. Amy passed on this insight about the female gut to her women friends. Although some were more accepting than others, she found that many of her friends had been having the same revelation. I guess God does work in mysterious ways.

Although some pooh-pooh the idea of spiritual healers, intuitive healers, card readers and mediums, Lynne did spend time with several of them. Their insight justified and honored her feelings, something she really needed at that time. Even though one healer offered the standard "this is only for the purpose of entertainment" mantra, Lynne knew that she was on the right path. Her Tarot card reading showed a new life coming her way with great health, happiness, and joy. Her dark knight was leaving, the cards said, and if she married him anytime in the next two years (ignoring this advice), her life would forever be doomed (strong entertainment words, I believe). She trusted her gut and moved on; the great health, happiness, and joy parts of her reading are still going strong in her life today. Another intuitive healer told Lynne that things in her life were improving as her sadness was peeling away like macadam ("just like the roads being repaired," as she put it) leading toward full healing. She was full of bright white energy beneath all her layers of sadness. Still another clairvoyant identified the black energy of her extremities only (feet and hands), as she saw her Mr. Wonderful leaving her life, moving on to offer his misery to another woman. Whether all of these ideas appeal to you or not, I can tell you that Lynne felt totally empowered and inspired by these healers. Today, she studies to be a sound healer, working with "singing bowls," tuning forks, and music, offering one more avenue of healing to those in need of something totally different.

Nancy, a schoolteacher friend, did some volunteer work at a rustic, set in nature, church camp and also became reacquainted with her faith. Her camp kids said it best when talking about following God's word. "If you don't do it, you will be in *big* trouble"! Who wants to be in trouble with the Big Guy/Gal? Not any of us. It is also easiest to go with the tried and true: that is God to me, to most of my friends. Nancy's faith, which she had temporarily lost when separating from her Mr. Wonderful, returned as she spoke to her church campers about having their pre-adolescent faith guide them through their life. She thought that she should do the same and she does her best to do that everyday. The campers had some really great sayings and one of them has stuck with her: FROG (Forever Rely on God).

Pray all that you can. My friend Bobby couldn't get enough guidance from above during this time. His rule of thumb was, pray when you wake up, when you are in the shower, when you eat breakfast, when you are on the way to work—you get the picture. Just the calmness of prayer settled and grounded him. He said you should feel free to yell during prayer, too, as he often did until one of his neighbors asked, "What is going on in there?" But he simply needed to release the frustration of the situation. When Bobby explained his present life situation and separation, all of his neighbors totally understood, many having gone through a similar turmoil in their own lives. And God will understand, too. Just remember to keep your eyes open if you try praying when driving! You do not need an accident and physical pain to compound your emotional hurt right now. Bobby often prayed out loud while driving, just pretending that he was singing along with the car radio. No one ever knew what he was really doing and he was happy with that.

And a few words from this feisty lady: Remember that God always answers prayers in Her own time, in Her own way, and in what is best for you, even though you may not feel that at this sad time.

Diamond

When in doubt about anything, always go to the highest power. The answers may not be what you expect or come when you expect them to, but they are still answers. Follow your gut and God will guide you in ways that you could never have imagined.

Section 5:

Moving On

The worst is behind you, but you can't just stand still and hope for the best. You need to take some positive actions to get that revitalized body, mind, and soul moving again in the right direction.

Chapter 14

Your New Social Life . . . Or at Least an Attempt at Having One

Since you really had no social life at all to speak of with Mr. Wonderful, now is the time to get one. You do deserve a life full of great people, great food, and, of course, great adventures. Right now you feel like crap, but eventually you will decide that you have seen enough of your four walls at home and that you need to see some new scenery. Get out there, by yourself if you have to, and experience the world. You'll be glad you did. These stories come from friends of friends and encompass all ages of women.

Jenny, a thirty-something executive, decided to go back to the time of her teens, when staying up all night, eating, and giggling was a fun evening. She thought, Why not repeat it? So she had a pajama party with six of her friends. As we ate ourselves silly, drank too much wine, and gabbed and gabbed, she did decide that she had truly missed being with her female friends who cared more about her than Mr. Wonderful ever did. While she did have a few male friends who wanted to come, she decided that females-only was best for now. That night did so much to lift her spirits that she planned to repeat this event with different themes at least twice a year, and maybe with a few males present (which definitely makes strip poker more fun).

Carol, a middle-aged medical professional, decided to do something special and have her own birthday party. Her birthday happened to fall around her first Christmas alone and she was dreading it intensely, so she did what any holiday birthday celebratee can easily do: she changed the date. One month later, in the doldrums of January, she held her first birthday party, for and in honor of her newly single self. Her Mr. Wonderful had never done this for her in 25 years of marriage. Carol had great snacks, foods, and her favorite, an ice cream cake, complete with candles and superb singing. "When you celebrate yourself, you can do it in any way that you want," she said. Next year's party is already in the planning stage and it's only August.

Invite family and friends for weekends and summer vacations. They love visiting and you need the company. The phone calls that Judy, a forty-something child advocate, received from family and friends had been a great help, but their visits were worth their weight in gold—or diamonds or pearls, if you prefer. She also got to do things with them, to go places that she might rather not go alone. Her house was full of love, people, and energy, a vibe that had been missing for years and years. Living so close to a major city offered her and her friends and family so much to do that plenty of items on her bucket list have been checked off.

Potluck dinners are also fun. Everybody brings her specialty. So what if you have only chocolate to eat? Every female loves chocolate. Annie, a retired music teacher, knew that she needed the conversation and laughing that these dinners offer, something that she could not get enough of in this year of recovery. "Rather to laugh than cry: all of us know that to be the case," she said. Just check out the newspaper events section and you can find many events such as these and never have to eat alone again. Even the local library sponsors cooking events. This is a great way to meet new people, too.

Going out with the girls: are you ready? Of course you are. It was a totally scary experience for Lorna as she ventured out with some single friends. She actually felt like she was cheating on Mr. Wonderful, even though *he* was the cheater in their 15-year relationship. Just watching all of the people was fun. Although she was still not ready to meet anyone, being out of the house was good for her. She looked great even if she did not feel so great inside. Lorna stayed out the entire evening on her first venture as a single woman, resisting the constant and overwhelming urge to drive home, run in the house, jump on the couch and pull the blanket over her head. To be honest, though, tears did follow as she realized that she really never expected to be out in this single mode ever again in her life. "Mr. Wonderful, you suck," she said often enough to get the anger and rage out of her system. Lorna now goes out regularly with her friends and has met some really interesting men.

Attend concerts and shows. Chris, a middle-aged researcher and amateur musician, went to her first concert solo and met some fascinating people. They were talkative, kind, and, probably seeing the sadness etched on her face, invited her to join them for a drink after the performance.

Turns out that they were musicians as well; they had a great deal in common and still meet at concerts today. Sometimes people do sense someone in a sad state and rise to the occasion. This was the case for Chris. I knew that she was recovering as she stood up with the rest of the crowd and danced in the aisles at a Broadway show performance. When was the last time that she did that? She couldn't remember, that's for sure, but reveled in her newly rediscovered love of theater.

Go to the gym. I mentioned this in an earlier chapter, but there's also a social element to exercise that deserves its own plug. For openers, Jill, a retired military officer, pictured her Mr. Wonderful's face in the racquetball court and aimed each shot at that visual. She just wacked away until his face finally disappeared. She got in shape and had the chance to ogle some really hot guys.

Theresa, a magazine editor, got in such great shape that she has begun running in 10K races. "Now that is an interesting crowd of people," she says. They are involved in fitness and nutrition just as she is. This sport also allows her to travel, which makes her wish that she had given more time and effort to her cheerleading days, now considered a sport in 36 states, even thought the 10K races are just as much fun, she says.

Diamond

Getting a social life means different things to different people. For me it was reconnecting with old friends and making new friends. I can only give you advice on what has worked for my friends and me. You may be ready to date again, but that has taken most of us a long time. As a matter of fact, I'm still working on that one. The subject of another book, I guess.

Chapter 15

My Vacation to Sedona

For every step I take,
For every person I meet
Cover me with your divine love
And protect me from all directions.
   Anonymous

This entire book so far has dealt with the actions and antics of many women who have taken traditional and some non-traditional steps to move on from their very own Mr. Wonderful partners. I, too, decided to complete the moving-on process by vacationing on my own in one of the most spiritually healing places in the world, Sedona, Arizona. A few friends had recommended this place after returning with positive healing accounts, so I decided to give it a try. Sedona is famous for a number of energy centers, or so-called "vortexes of subtle energy." (For some reason, the Sedonans call them vortexes rather than the more common *vortices*). The energy from these vortexes emanates from the whole area around Sedona, and can be noticed in subtle ways anywhere in the town. But I was told that if you travel to the actual vortex sites, where the energy is strongest, that it will be an even more uplifting experience. The energy you take from the vortexes remains with you and will affect you positively for many days and months to come.

So, what's an energy vortex, you ask? I knew that a vortex is funnel-shaped and can be made up of anything that flows, such as wind, water, or electricity. But the vortexes in Sedona are swirling centers of subtle energy coming out from the surface of the earth. According to one account I found online, "The vortex energy is not exactly electricity or magnetism, although it does leave a slight measurable residual magnetism in the places where it is strongest. The energy resonates with and strengthens the Inner Being of each person that comes within about a quarter to a half mile of it."

Whatever the reason, because of these vortexes Sedona has long been known as a spiritual power center that has attracted vast numbers of people who are "on the path", having made a commitment to grow spiritually. It's also why a large New Age community has sprung up in the Sedona area, and why it has sometimes been called a "spiritual Disneyland". I've nothing against the New Age, so I decided to follow my friends' advice and see if I could change my energy by spending some time there.

I rolled into Phoenix on a steaming hot July day, although I was told that the heat that day was mild—a mere 98 degrees. I am still wondering about that concept because it was pretty much like walking into a blast furnace. (I do understand from some of the natives that temperatures in the 120-degree range can cook hot dogs in foil on the sidewalk. Wow). Wondering how I would cope with this heat, I was pleased to learn that Sedona itself is cooler; it was, but just barely. T-shirts lettered with "It's only dry heat" were ever-present. The accompanying drawing was of a skeleton.

As we drove from Phoenix to Sedona, the rocks and the land changed dramatically, which made me think about how we all transform in the same way as we move on with life. The transition from plain limestone to the vibrant Sedona red dirt described pretty accurately how I had felt earlier in my life. I was hopeful that those bland feelings of discontent would revert back to the more normal fiery red of my personality after my sojourn to Sedona. Many places were on the travel docket: as many red rocks as possible, any rocks, national parks, and as many healing experiences as I could handle.

I chose to take a workshop designed to explore all of the spiritual settings in the Sedona area, offering attendees a chance to work on harnessing that spiritual energy. It included a walk-about to some of the special vortex areas that promised to provide me with the energy I needed to move on and become more connected with my own inner spirit. I wanted to be healed, to forgive, and to live my life with a renewed energy and awareness of Spirit. A friend who is a third-generation healer, medium, seer, and spiritual guide accompanied me, and I knew that she would provide a life-changing experience as I completed this journey with her.

Numerous friends had told me that certain vortex locations in Sedona had a remarkable healing effect, so I decided to seek out as many of them as I had time to visit. There are four of these special areas, but one of the most powerful was said to be Cathedral Rock, and I began my journey there. These towering red rock cliffs have a church right below called the Chapel of the Holy Cross, which was built in 1956. You can go inside and start your journey with a prayer. The Cathedral Rock section of the vortex included a hike, the construction of a promise/prayer altar, and a dip in the water. I was instructed to pile five stones on top of each other in order of decreasing size. Each rock was to symbolize a promise/prayer for one's life; for me the promises were for a new life, filled with joy, healing, and gratitude for all of the great things that I already had. The area was teeming with promise altars, as so many visitors were making promises for their present and future lives. The splash in the water was intended as a respite from the heat of the hike as well as a kind of baptism to shed the past and move on to a new future.

Moments spent in that cathedral area set the tone for my entire trip. I felt a calm like never before. Peace. Quiet. Stillness. Curiously enough, just to the left of the cathedral was the Snoopy Rock, which provided a humorous moment. God surely does have a sense of humor. My faith and humor also have been my two biggest assets in life, so these two sites were good omens for this trip. I knew at that very moment that I would never want to leave. (But since we all need to work for a living, eventually I *would* have to leave).

Heading north to the Wupatki and Sunset Crater Volcano Park, I was, once again, overwhelmed by the natural beauty of the area. To journey there, however, we had to travel through the Sedona Valley, which was filled with trees scarred from the recent forest fires, even as new trees and shrubbery seemed to be emerging everywhere. Many trails and sites were closed still to be repaired from the extensive recent fire damage of the previous month. I could not visit Slide Rock and speed down the rocks into the water below as I had wanted, but I was still able to walk in an 800-year-old, 16-mile-long lava flow. How any ruins had survived this was beyond me, but there they were. A pueblo complete with two fire circles, adjoining buildings, and a naturally air-conditioned blowhole were still standing. Beyond the pueblo was the Painted Desert area, whose stones were transformed from the heat of the lava flow into some of the most beautiful and unusual colors of rocks anywhere in the United States. Thousands of Native Americans perished in the lava flow that had damaged so much of the land, and yet the beauty left behind was sensational. Sounds like my journey, doesn't it? I was damaged by the hurt in my life, but I am emerging like the new vegetation of the land with more clarity, purpose, and vitality than I ever thought possible.

Further on at the Lava Rock Cave, which was also carved out from this lava flow, we hiked down into the cave itself. Its wide-open floor area was called the underground cathedral. I was again seeing the parallels in my life: the damage, the regrowth, and the beauty re-entering my life. Re-growing and reviving were the cycle of the land and my life cycle, too. No wonder I felt a special kinship to this area; the land reflected my feelings, thoughts, and journey.

Throughout my travels there, I encountered many Native American vendors who were selling their wares. One particular group of vendors was donating their profits to programs to benefit the young members of their tribes who live on the reservations helping to regrow and revitalize their traditions, too. Seems that so many of us are in a rebuilding mode. This was another kinship that I felt with the land and its people.

As I arose each morning, I took a walk and absorbed the grandeur of the mountains. A gentle breeze surrounded me everywhere I went, even when the surrounding trees were not moving. That must have been the energy everyone was talking about. I felt calm and yet full of energy. How's that for a post-menopausal woman? Those were not words I would have used to describe myself before then, yet that is exactly how I felt in this vortex area of healing. To move forward and to live my life to the fullest was my healing goal. However, I did spend more time than I thought I would in tears, letting go of the past. That was a reaction shared by some of my friends who visited this area as well. I have not had a cry like that in a long time, but felt so calm after I let my tears flow.

For a change of pace we took a day trip from Sedona to the South Rim of the Grand Canyon, which also happens to be in Arizona and not that far away. I had been there years before and the scenery was even more breathtaking than I remembered. You can walk through many sections of the park, but the shuttles made the heat-filled journey much easier. Great energy was everywhere; I never felt lonely, even though I did walk alone through many sections of the park. Since I have trouble with heights, peering over the rails was a tentative move for me. Still, I felt totally safe doing this and I dreamed that night that I was flying through the Grand Canyon on the back on an eagle. I had not ingested any weird foods or plants that day, so how does one explain that? According to a native healer that I visited during my vacation, the eagle is one of my power animals, along with the butterfly, swan, elk, wolf, and horse that are all akin to me. I vividly remember the dream flight and how freeing it felt.

Among the other vortices that my friends had told me about, besides Cathedral Rock they had especially singled out Airport Vortex and Bell Rock as places that would change me. The energy there, they insisted, would offer me a chance to move on, to heal, a return to my true self. I would feel more alive and healthy than ever before, and my liveliness would be increased in ways that I could only imagine. The Airport Vortex included all of the vistas of the vortex and astonishing views of the Sedona Valley. Calming energy surrounded me as I lifted my arms to gather in the healing energy. No one told me to do this, but I it seemed to be the right thing to do. I do this now every day.

Sitting quietly at Bell Rock was the beginning of my total healing. Right before dusk seemed like the best time to visit this rock, where so many of my friends had said they just "let it fly", a place where screaming and yelling was helping people release their sorrows, hurts, and sadness. Seated on a beach towel facing the horizon toward the setting sun, I rested in a yoga pose and the chakra clearing began. As you may know, the chakras are our inner centers of subtle energy, and the subtle energies of the vortexes are said to interact with and enhance our internal chakra energy. As instructed by my friend, the medium and healer, I settled in with my breathing and repeated, "I am receiving prayers of healing and the energy of healing". Even in the stillness, a breeze was shortly surrounding me. I saw the healing colors of blue, blue-green, and yellow representing the spirit of Christ, and white flashes representing the Great Spirit. The circles that she traced in my palms increased the energy flow around my body. Blockages were cleared and I sat up in a dizzy, yet euphoric, state. My throat chakra seemed to be sensitive to my speaking, so I sat as quietly as I could. The energy of my feet began to buzz (a sensation that continued for several days). After sitting through the setting of the sun, I felt a lightness, openness, and peacefulness that had eluded me for many years. With a bit of help, I could finally let it all go.

I had read that the natural beauty of our world is created by the four elements of water, fire, earth, and air. All of those elements lined up for me when I visited these vortex locations, enhancing the energy of my body and enabling me to feel more happiness, to gain more insight into my thoughts, to clear out physical and emotional hurts, and to start a new journey in my life. I physically looked and felt better than I ever had in my life. I was totally stunned by the effects I felt after visiting these sites.

I continue to enjoy these feelings even today. I would never have believed that I could feel like this unless I had experienced it myself. This Sedona vacation changed my entire life. After my experiences there, I felt ready to begin a new chapter. I have always felt that living well is the best revenge and I am ready to do that now. I wish the same for all of my feisty lady friends. It will take true grit to move on. You will need perseverance, a determination to overcome obstacles. You will also need the commitment to make a conscious choice to do this. And finally you need passion, a positive attitude, and a will to move on even though you may not want to. All of these gritty qualities are necessary for you to meet your goal of surviving Mr. Wonderful. I expected that I would recover from him and I did. And so can you.

Acknowledgments

Special thanks to all contributors namely my Mom, feisty friends, the Vintage Ladies, relatives, acquaintances, TV talk show hosts, magazines, and comedians for their contributions to this book.
The names are too many to record here.
Keep those stories coming.
Stay tuned for Book 2!